GHOSTHUNTING
SOUTHERN
NEW ENGLAND

AMERICA'S
HAUNTED ROAD TRIP

Titles in the *America's Haunted Road Trip* Series:

GHOSTHUNTING
SOUTHERN
NEW ENGLAND

ANDREW LAKE

CLERISY PRESS

Ghosthunting Southern New England

For further information, contact the publisher at:
Clerisy Press
An imprint of AdventureKEEN
306 Greenup Street
Covington, KY 41011
www.clerisypress.com

LIBRARY OF CONGRESS CATALOGING-IN-PUBLICATION DATA

Lake, Andrew (Andrew S.), 1964–
    Ghosthunting Southern New England / by Andrew Lake.
    — 1st ed.
        p. cm. — (America's haunted road trip)
    ISBN-13: 978-1-57860-487-6 (pbk.); ISBN-10: 1-57860-487-7
    ISBN 978-1-57860-488-3 (ebook);
    ISBN 978-1-57860-616-0 (hardcover)
    1. Haunted places—New England. 2. Ghosts—New
England. I. Title. II. Series.

    BF1472.U6L35 2011
    133.10974—dc23

                                            2011027240

Distributed by Publishers Group West
Printed in the United States of America
First edition, first printing

Editor: Donna Poehner
Cover design: Scott McGrew
Cover and interior photos provided by the author unless
    otherwise noted

To my mother, Alicia, who told me years ago that I should write a book about haunted places, and to my late father, Arthur, who never believed one word about ghosts

TABLE OF CONTENTS

Rhode Island 75

Connecticut 139

Acknoweldgments

THIS BOOK WAS MADE POSSIBLE by kind help and input from the following people: John Kachuba, Jeff Belanger, Donna Poehner, Jim Ignasher, John Zaffis, and Matt Moniz. Thanks to all my friends and colleagues who helped me look for "different" haunted places to write about: Pamela Patalano, Kimberly Hopkins, Kathy Caslin, Eric LaVoie, Ron Kolek, Tim Weisberg, Tom Laughlin, and Charles Reis. Many thanks to Arlene Nicholson and Tony D'Agostino for inviting me along to investigate the John York House, Hail Homestead, and Captain Grant's. Special gratitude to all the groups, societies, and individuals that assisted with the research: The Foster Preservation Society (Rhode Island), the ladies at the Foster Town Hall, Killingly Historical and Genealogical Society (Connecticut), the Greenville Public Library (Rhode Island), R. I. S. E. U. P., Viola Ulm, Ed Robinson, Donna Mooney, Pat Morgan, Christopher Balzano, Dan Gordon, Gary Joseph, and all the wonderful people throughout southern New England who invited me into their fine establishments to hear some amazing ghost stories.

Preface

Do you believe in ghosts?

If you are like 52 percent of Americans (according to a recent Harris Poll), you *do* believe that ghosts walk among us. Perhaps you have heard your name called in a dark and empty house. It could be that you have awoken to the sound of footsteps outside your bedroom door, only to find no one there. It is possible that you saw your grandmother sitting in her favorite rocking chair, the same grandmother who had passed away several years before. Maybe you took a photo of a crumbling, deserted farmhouse and discovered strange mists and orbs in the photo, anomalies that were not visible to your naked eye.

If you have experienced similar paranormal events, then you know that ghosts exist. Even if you have not yet experienced these things, you are curious about the paranormal world, the spirit realm. If you weren't, you would not now be reading this Preface to the latest book in the *America's Haunted Road Trip* series from Clerisy Press.

Over the last several years, I have investigated haunted locations across the country and with each new site, I found myself becoming more fascinated with ghosts. What are they? How do they manifest themselves? Why are they here? These are just a few of the questions I have been asking. No doubt, you have been asking the same questions.

The books in the *America's Haunted Road Trip* series can help you find the answers to your questions about ghosts. We've gathered together some of America's top ghost writers (no pun intended) and researchers and asked them to write about their states' favorite haunts. Each location that they write about is open to the public so that you can visit it for yourself and try out your ghosthunting skills. In addition to telling you about their often hair-raising adventures, the writers have included maps and travel directions so that you can take your own haunted roadtrip.

People may think that southern New England is nothing more than rolling green hills, quaint little village greens, and miles of rocky beaches, but Andrew Lake's *Ghosthunting Southern New England* proves that the hills are home to shadowy entities that are seen only for an instant before disappearing among the trees and spirits that frequent old weathered cemeteries on the village greens. The book is a spine-tingling trip through Connecticut, Massachusetts, and Rhode Island with stops at inns, old mills, historic sites, and cemeteries—all of them haunted.

Ride shotgun with Andrew as he seeks out the ghosts of witches, suicides, and murder victims at Rhode Island's Hopkins Mills. Travel with him to North Adams, Massachusetts, where the sorrowful ghost of John Widders can be seen standing in a window of the Houghton Mansion, the place in which he worked as a servant and where he was responsible for the accidental death of two women, or sit for a spell in the steamboat-styled home of Mark Twain in Hartford, Connecticut, and see if you can spot the playful ghosts of the famous writer's daughters as they flit through the house. And can that ghostly voice that called *I will be right down* at the Nathan Hale Homestead in Connecticut be the ghost of Richard Hale, the father of the American spy Nathan Hale? Hang on tight; *Ghosthunting Southern New England* is a scary ride.

But once you've finished reading this book, don't unbuckle your seatbelt. There are still forty-nine states left for your haunted road trip! See you on the road!

John Kachuba
Editor, *America's Haunted Road Trip*

GHOSTHUNTING
Southern
NEW ENGLAND

Massachusetts

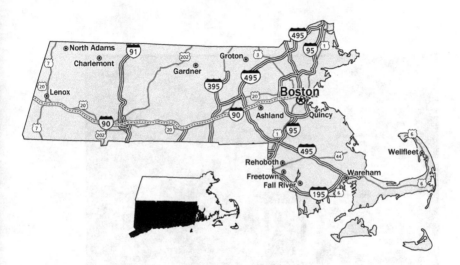

Ashland
Stone's Public House

Charlemont
The Charlemont Inn

Fall River
Lizzie Borden Bed-and-Breakfast/
Museum

Freetown
The Freetown State Forest

Gardner
The Victorian

Groton
The Groton Inn

Lenox
Ventfort Hall Mansion and Gilded
Age Museum

North Adams
The Houghton Mansion

Quincy
USS *Salem*

Rehoboth
Anawan Rock

Wareham
The Fearing Tavern

Wellfleet
The Inn at Duck Creeke

CHAPTER 1

Inn at Duck Creeke

WELLFLEET, MASSACHUSETTS

The Saltworks House

CAPE COD IS CONSIDERED BY MANY to be one of the most haunted locations in all of New England. The history of the Cape and the people who have lived there is older than America itself. It is a history full of hardships and tales of survival from the unforgiving elements, disease, and men with hostile intentions. The older generation on Cape Cod feels strongly that their ghosts are human souls who have chosen to stay within a place they had a strong connection to in life. These Yankees also believe the "old wood," as they call it, is imprinted with spiritual energy from Cape Cod's past. For many years in

New England it was common practice to disassemble old buildings and use the wood to build additions onto existing structures. People on Cape Cod have been recycling their wood for hundreds of years. Because of this frugal practice, the old-timers say there are buildings throughout the Cape that have inherited ghosts along with the "old wood" taken from the spirit's original residence.

Wellfleet was established in 1763, although the first permanent settlement there was founded in 1650. What brought the early settlers to this part of the outer Cape was the abundance of fish in Cape Cod Bay. Today, Wellfleet Harbor is still a busy port for fisherman and is well known for its oysters. In 1961, Wellfleet became part of the Cape Cod National Seashore Park. More than 60 percent of the town is within this preserve, thus protecting it from over-development and allowing the town to keep its identity with the past.

The Inn at Duck Creeke is one of the town's unspoiled landmarks. Located on Main Street, the inn was originally built in 1810 as a home for a sea captain and his family. An inlet from Cape Cod Bay once existed that allowed the sea captain to steer his ship inland and dock close to his home. A causeway built in the early twentieth century for the railroad has since turned the inlet into a salt-water marsh. A tidal creek now runs through the marsh, creating a duck pond on the back side of the property. In the first part of the twentieth century, a gentleman named Joe Price made many renovations to the inn and its adjacent buildings. Price made good use of buildings that were left abandoned around the Wellfleet area. Every piece that could be salvaged from those structures was used to make repairs and additions to the inn. He didn't let any of that "old wood" go to waste.

The Inn at Duck Creeke is actually made up of four separate buildings. Along with the Captain's House, there are three other buildings that occupy the five wooded acres. They are named

The Saltworks House, The Tavern, and Carriage House. The tavern building is referred to as "The Hodge Podge" because it is made up of sections of homes from the seventeenth and eighteenth centuries. This uniquely styled building houses both the Sweet Seasons and The Duck Creeke Tavern restaurants.

The Duck Creeke Tavern is the oldest existing tavern in Wellfleet. The current owners of the inn are Bob Morrill and Judy Pihl. Bob and Judy first became associated with the inn in the mid-1970s when they were leasing the Sweet Seasons restaurant. In 1980, they bought the inn. Shortly after Bob and Judy had settled into the property, the ghosts made their presence known to them.

It was December 1980—the couple's first winter on the property. They were living in The Saltworks House, which is located about one hundred feet from the back of the Captain's House. Bob and Judy were getting ready to prepare their first lobster dinner in their "new" home. Judy needed a large pot to cook the lobsters in so she sent Bob to retrieve one from the kitchen of the Sweet Seasons restaurant. It was a cold, dark night as he walked up the lane, flashlight in hand, and entered the kitchen from the back of the restaurant. Bob recalls, "I was walking through the kitchen and a large, metal, one-gallon measuring can flew off the shelf. It didn't fall on the floor; it flew all the way across the kitchen in front of me and then rolled another twenty feet. I grabbed the pot and went back home to Judy and said, 'That's the last time I'll go in there after dark, alone!'"

The ghost of Eulalia Price, Joe's wife, may have been responsible for that flying piece of kitchenware. People who remember Eulalia say she was a serious, hardworking woman. She managed the hospitality side of the inn's business and was responsible for booking all the entertainment. Mrs. Price was from New York and had a background in the theater. Well into the early 1970s, she wore long, old-fashion dresses that were starched and

The Duck Creeke Tavern is haunted by the spirits of two musicians who died while performing on the tavern's stage.

ironed to perfection. A woman who worked for Mrs. Price told Judy Phil that Eulalia was the kind of manager who would line her staff up for inspection and count the number of peas on the plates. "She was a strong character. This was her place; this still is her place," says Judy.

Mrs. Price is believed to be the woman in white who has been seen at the restaurant and its kitchen. Judy saw her ghost one afternoon in the lobby area of the restaurant. She says, "I just happened to be walking through the kitchen, looking out towards the lobby and something caught my eye. I took two steps back. I then watched a very diminutive woman float from one side, with the sun behind her, cross the lobby and back again, and then disappear. It was three-dimensional, you could almost see through it and it was female." Judy finishes by saying, "It was a very interesting moment."

At the other end of the "Hodge Podge" is The Duck Creeke Tavern. Even though these two restaurants are attached, there seems to be a different group of ghosts in The Tavern Room. Over the years, Bob has learned of three deaths that occurred on the property. Two of those deaths happened inside the Tavern Room. Years ago, when the tavern was called The Chart Room, a husband-and-wife musical act used to play there regularly. One night while they were performing, the wife died on stage. The late singer's husband would come to the Tavern Room in his later years and just sit and watch the stage. He would never order anything to eat or drink; he wouldn't even ask for a glass of water. Judy used to wonder if maybe he could see his wife on the stage. A female ghost has been seen around the Tavern Room, and most feel that it is her spirit.

Musicians have reported hearing a woman singing while they were performing. One night when a piano player was on stage, Bob noticed that he was moving his head around and swatting at the air with his right hand. When he took a short break, Bob asked him why he was jerking his head and waving his hand around. He looked at Bob very seriously and said, "Because she was pulling my hair!"

Oddly enough, the woman's death isn't the only one to have played out on the tavern's stage. A piano player also passed away suddenly while performing. If this pianist is haunting the stage, he might be responsible for the microphones and amplifiers being turned off while musicians are playing.

The third death known to have taken place on the property was first reported to Bob and Judy by one of their former waiters, a young Irishman named Eugene, who was a "sensitive" who could feel and see things that others could not. One vision in particular that he told his employers about was seeing a man hanging himself from a large locust tree in back of the tavern. Bob had cut the locust tree down ten years before this young man had started working for them. In June of 2010, an old man stopped by the Tavern Room and while reminiscing about the summers he had spent in Wellfleet as a boy, he mentioned that his college roommate's father had hanged himself from a tree on the property. Bob and Judy said they had never doubted Eugene, especially when he told them that their inn was haunted by many ghosts.

The Saltworks House is the oldest building on the property. It was built in the early 1700s and was originally located by the harbor. The house is named for the grinding stones that were taken from an old salt mill and used to make its front walk and steps. The couple no longer lives in the house; it now contains five small guest rooms. During the years they did live there, Judy said she would sometimes hear the sound of someone walking around, softly, upstairs. On more than a few occasions she heard what sounded like beads from a broken necklace, bouncing across the floor, but she could never find the source.

One season, some guests who were staying on the ground floor of the Saltworks House, complained about the patter of little feet in the room above theirs. Another time, a couple had commented on hearing a baby crying in one of the upstairs rooms. A check of the inn's register and a quick word with the staff confirmed that there were no infants or children staying in the Saltworks House when these sounds were heard.

The Captain's House has at least three ghosts, and they seem to be the friendliest of all the phantoms. Bob and Judy are pretty sure they are the wife and two daughters of the sea captain who lived in the house. As far as anyone knows, the two daughters were seen only once, but are often heard moving about on the second floor. The Captain's wife is reported to appear as a beautiful woman in white and also appears to be a kind soul. In the early 1980s, a female guest awoke with a scream when she found a strange woman in her room. This woman glided across the bedroom, through the furniture and up to the guest. She then placed her hand on the frightened woman's shoulder and said, "Don't worry, everything will be all right." The guest was able to go back to sleep, but checked out in the morning.

About a year after that incident, the inn got a phone call from a couple who recently had stayed in The Captain's House with their four-year-old daughter. They wanted to know the identity of the woman whom their child kept talking about. The young girl told her parents that a nice lady, dressed in white, had talked to her in their room. This woman wanted to make sure the little girl was taking her medicine. The couple couldn't understand this because their daughter was not on any medication. The bemused innkeepers told the couple about the other guest's encounter and left it at that. As Judy says, "Our ghosts seem very comfortable here, and we are comfortable with them."

CHAPTER 2

Fearing Tavern Museum
WAREHAM, MASSACHUSETTS

"WELCOME TO WAREHAM. Gateway to Cape Cod." That is what a decorative sign declares at the edge of town, on Route 28 East. Most modern maps show Cape Cod as starting east of the canal, but the folks of Wareham strongly beg to differ on that notion. Setting all local debate aside, it can be agreed that Wareham is one of the oldest settled areas in Massachusetts and if a long history of human habitation is truly an ingredient for ghostly activity, it would explain why the town is so haunted.

Friends and colleagues who grew up in Wareham have brought to my attention about half a dozen private homes and businesses they know through family, friends, and their

9

The haunted rocking chair

own personal experiences are very haunted. One such ghost is believed to be the original owner of the Tremont Nail Company; he has been seen walking from the front of the factory to the little shop across Elm Street. The nail company is the oldest manufacturer of hand-cut nails in the United States, and the little shop was originally its company store.

Nearby, on the Cranberry Highway (Route 28), stands the fifties-style Mill Pond Diner. It is the third diner to occupy the location since the 1920s. One of the cooks, Timmy, who has been working there for sixteen years, told me that he and some of his fellow employees have seen a fast-moving form enter the back of the diner and move down the stairs to the cellar. A psychic visited the roadside eatery and claimed that there are spirits walking back and forth from the cemetery on the other side of the highway to the Fearing Tavern, which is directly in back of the diner. She said they are just passing through because the diner is in their way.

The land on which the nail factory, the company store, and the diner are located was originally owned by Isaac Bump, the miller, who built a simple, two-room house on the land in 1690. Isaac ran three gristmills, and as time went on the Bump family grew, bought land, and eventually became involved in the iron industry. Over time the Bumps sold off their holdings and moved away to follow prosperity elsewhere. (An interesting side note to the Bump family is that one of their descendents was Mercy Lavinia Warren Bump—aka Mrs. Tom Thumb).

Israel Fearing bought the three-and-one-half acre plot and its little house from Isaac Bump. In 1765 the Fearings added an upstairs floor. Sometime around 1774 it became known as the Fearing Tavern. Further additions were made in 1820, making a total of sixteen rooms. The house and land would stay in the Fearing family for two hundred years. It would also play an important part in the history of Wareham.

The old Boston Post Road, known today as Elm Street, ran right in front of the Fearing Tavern. Stagecoaches would stop here and unload their weary travelers for food, drink, and a place to spend the night. The tavern's Tap Room, or Publik Room, was not only a place for passengers to refresh themselves, but also a place for town business to be discussed by Wareham's selectmen. Grog, the common drink in those days, was served to the town officials during these meetings at the taxpayers' expense. People were not the only important cargo carried by the stagecoaches; mail was also delivered and picked up here, making the tavern also the town's post office. The small room that served as the post master's office is still in place on the first floor as is the well-restored Tap Room.

From the early 1940s to the late 1950s, the Akins family owned the property and ran the aptly named Akins Diner. They also lived in the old Fearing homestead while running their business. No one from the Akins family will go on record about whether anything "strange" went on in the old tavern while they lived there, but locals say they have heard rumors of such happenings.

In 1957 Ernie Blanchard bought the tavern and adjacent diner from the Akins family. Ernie replaced the original wooden diner for an O'Mahoney model, but found it too small, so he changed it out for the larger one that is there today. The Blanchards chose not to live in the Fearing Tavern because it was badly in need of repair and had no modern conveniences, although they appreciated the significance of the historic building and felt it should be saved. In 1958 Mr. Blanchard donated the tavern to the Wareham Historical Society and so began the difficult task of polishing this amazing gem.

A successful campaign to raise funds allowed the historical society to hire building contractors skilled in the art of restoring old homes. Their talents are evident the moment one approaches and enters the building. All the rooms are furnished with eighteenth- and nineteenth-century pieces, some of which are original to the home. The tavern is almost exactly the way it was in the days the Fearing family owned it. There is no plumbing and only a few electric lights. The museum has a telephone, but it is well hidden from view and is only used for necessary communications. Some of the best paranormal investigators in southern New England believe the Fearing Tavern holds more than just material objects from its past. This writer agrees.

On the evening of September 24, 2008, the historical society allowed the hosts of Spooky Southcoast Radio to conduct the first-ever paranormal investigation of the Fearing Tavern Museum. The host of the program, Tim Weisberg, and his science advisor, Matt Moniz, invited along an expert in electronic voice phenomenon (EVP for short) named Mike Markowicz, as well as local paranormal enthusiast Carlston Wood and me to help out. Earlier in the evening, I hung out with the team at the diner to hear tales of strange happenings in the old tavern. Besides whispers that the Atkins family had experiences they kept to themselves, I was told about unearthly lights seen mov-

The Toy Room. A strange little light was captured on infrared video coming out of the wall on the left and traveling to the dolls on the shelf.

ing about the building when it was unoccupied. Those who witnessed these lights did not believe that the energy producing the brightness was nothing more than flashlights used by people exploring the empty house.

Carlston Wood's daughter, Ashley, stopped by to tell us about an exceptional moment she and a girlfriend shared one summer afternoon while on a guided tour of the museum. The two teenaged girls were taking up the rear as the tour group exited one of the upstairs bedrooms, their guide leading the way. They both turned to take one last look at the room, and as they turned back to walk through the doorway, their eyes met. "I think we must have had the same expression on our faces. We turned to look back into the room and she was gone, but the rocking chair was still moving. We looked at each other without saying a word and then we caught up with the group downstairs." They later told the guide what they had seen; the translucent form of an old woman, sitting in the rocking chair, knitting. The guide told the two girls she believed them and left it at that.

As for our team's investigation that night, we did not go home disappointed. We felt honored to be given first crack at catching any evidence (or as we like to call it, data) that could back up the claims that the tavern is haunted. Just to be allowed into this fantastic museum, at night, with all our equipment, was a thrill in itself. We were, of course, not left alone in the tavern. A member of the historical society, Carol McMarrow, was there to keep an eye on things, just in case. When you see for yourself the wonderful antiques held within the place, you will understand why. In addition to Carolyn, a few other people from the society dropped by to check out the investigation.

After we had taken in the whole layout of the house, members of the team and the folks from the historical society took a walk down Elm Street to see the Tremont Nail Company. The only living souls left behind were Matt Moniz, Carolyn, and I. Since the house was now quiet, I took the opportunity to conduct an EVP session in one of the upstairs bedrooms. Matt and Carolyn were downstairs talking about the society's need for volunteers. Later, when the audio recording was played back, the unmistakable sound of someone "shushing" Matt and Carolyn could be heard. It happened right as the two of them were speaking at the same time.

The other interesting bit of data caught by my equipment was a strange, flickering ball of light. I had placed a video camera recorder on infrared in the small room above the Tap Room. This was where the tavern would have stored spirits for the bar. The museum uses it to display period-piece toys and dolls. More than an hour into the recording, a small, almost shimmering light came out of the wall, moved slowly through the air, and went into an antique doll on a shelf. All who have seen the footage agree that it is not dust, nor is it a bug. It is just plain weird.

Whenever I consider this pixie-like light I can't help thinking about one of the startling class A (meaning absolutely clear) EVPs recorded by Mike Markowicz that night. It is the voice of a young girl asking, "Wanna play dress up?"

Some believe the building's confusing architecture, created over the years by the several additions to the original house, was used to hide escaping slaves on the Underground Railroad. There is even a tale of a British soldier who hid in the house from the local militia by taking advantage of a space found on the second floor, between the first and second structures. It has also been said there was a tunnel which led from the tavern's cellar to the Tremont Nail Company. In 1977 the founder of the Wareham Historical Society, the late Raymond A. Rider, recorded his doubts about the Fearing Tavern being used as a station on the Underground Railroad. He also stated that he and the builders found no evidence of a tunnel during the restoration. However, another EVP recorded by Mike makes us wonder if the tales are really true after all. It is a male voice with a slight southern accent saying, "We got'em mouse holes in here." The term "mouse hole" can sometimes mean a place of hiding.

Towards the end of the night, Tim, Mike, and I were in the attic using a "ghost box," which is nothing more than a digital radio, altered to constantly scan the AM band. The theory behind this device is that it lets one hear EVPs live as they are captured, instead of waiting later to listen to an audio recording. I am skeptical about this method of catching spirit voices, but what we heard come out of the radio's speaker made our jaws drop. While getting some intriguing responses to Tim's questions, I stepped in and asked, "Are we talking to a red man or a white man?" and the almost immediate response was, "Black woman." As ghosthunters and New Englanders, the team and I all agree that the haunted Fearing Tavern is one of our favorite locations.

CHAPTER 3

The Lizzie Borden Bed-and-Breakfast/Museum

FALL RIVER, MASSACHUSETTS

ON AUGUST 4, 1892, the city of Fall River, Massachusetts, became the center of media attention when the bodies of Andrew Borden and his wife, Abby, were found brutally murdered in their home at 92 Second Street. It is believed that the killer used a hatchet to mutilate the heads of both victims. Investigators concluded that Mrs. Borden was attacked from behind in an upstairs bedroom, and Andrew was assaulted a short time later while he was taking an afternoon nap on a sofa downstairs. Mr. Borden's youngest daughter from a previous marriage, Lizzie, told the authorities she had discovered the ghastly crime scene after returning from the barn, which was located in back of the house. The police found discrepancies in her story and arrested Lizzie for the murders. Even though a large majority in the community felt that she was guilty, Miss Borden was acquitted a year later by a jury of twelve men. The Borden case has since become the second-most-infamous, unsolved murder mystery of the Victorian era, next to London's notorious Jack the Ripper.

The Borden home stands today as the only witness to the horrible crimes perpetrated within its walls. For more than one hundred years, theories and allegations about the Bordens and their way of life have led many researchers to reexamine the case in a nearly obsessive attempt to solve these murders. A myriad of books, magazines, newspaper articles, and documentaries have presented a number of different theories as to the identity and motives of the person, or persons, responsible for the deaths of Mr. and Mrs. Borden. It seems more than likely the world will never really know exactly what happened on that warm summer day and why.

Lizzie Borden and her sister, Emma, left their family home after the trial and moved into a new, modern house on French Street, which they named Maplecroft. Lizzie lived the life of a spinster and died from pneumonia at the age of sixty-seven. She was buried in the family plot in the city's Oak Grove Cemetery. The house on Second Street changed ownership a few times after the Borden sisters' departure. In 1948 the property was purchased by the McGinn family. It remained their private home until 1994, when Mrs. McGinn passed away. Her granddaughter, Martha McGinn, bought the house with her partner, Ron Evans, and they had the place converted into a bed-and-breakfast, which opened for business in 1996. The McGinn family had experienced paranormal activity in the old house throughout the time it was their family home, but Martha's and Ron's intent was to let the story of Lizzie Borden be the draw for their novel B&B. However, over the eight years in which they ran the place, the ghosts did make themselves known to the staff and guests. The word got out; the old Borden place is haunted.

Lee-Ann Wilbur and her partner, Donald Woods, bought the Lizzie Borden Bed-and-Breakfast/Museum in June, 2004. Lee-Ann had heard stories about the place being haunted, but didn't let it bother her. It only took about a week in the house before she had her first unnerving encounter. Lee-Ann went downstairs to the basement and as she stepped off the bottom step, she walked into an intense cold spot. The rest of the cellar felt as warm as the June day, but that one spot was horribly cold. As Lee-Ann stood there trying to make sense of the isolated patch of cold air, she felt the sensation of someone running a finger down her back. That was enough to make her leave the basement for the rest of the day.

The basement does have its share of creepy stories. The dry sink in which Lizzie may have washed off the blood evidence is located in a niche below the kitchen. Long before Andrew and Abby were murdered, Lizzie is said to have chopped off the head of her stepmother's cat on a wooden table that the Bordens' kept in the basement as a butcher's block. Abby's cat is believed to haunt the house. Some guests of the B&B have made comments at breakfast about a cat that jumped up on their bed in the middle of the night. A photograph taken in the kitchen appears to have captured the cat's ghost, peering around the side of the stove. A shadowy figure has also been seen in the basement, darting quickly out of sight. One witness said it had a female form.

The most impressive tale from the basement has to be the night that four of my friends and colleagues, Chris Balzano, Matt Moniz, Jeff Belanger, and Tim Weisberg, all heard the unmistakable sound of children running and laughing on the first floor above them. The doors were locked, and they were

Lizzie Borden

the only people in the house that night. When the four of them went to investigate, they could find no one. Three children were drowned by their mother years ago on the property next door. Perhaps their ghosts visit the house from time to time. Lee-Ann told me that she has caught glimpses of shadow figures all throughout the house. One night in particular, she had fallen asleep on the couch in the front parlor.

There were no guests in the house that night, so she slept soundly until about three o'clock in the morning when she awoke to the sound of taxicab drivers talking outside on the street. As she became aware of her surroundings and the time, she noticed that the light bulbs on the chandelier were glowing dimmer and dimmer. The bulbs then went out completely. At that very moment, she noticed a female figure in a long dress, standing at the foot of the front hall stairs. Before Lee-Ann could react, the figure moved quickly up the stairs to the second floor without making a sound. "I grabbed my blanket and went out-side to sleep in my car," said Lee-Ann. As she went out the back

Lizzie Borden's sawing machine

door she told the ghost, "You win, I'm out of here!"

Matt Moniz has been investigating the paranormal for more than twenty-five years. He works as a chemist by day and acts as the science advisor for Spooky Southcoast Radio. Lee-Ann Wilbur notifies him whenever anything strange happens in the house. She also has Matt conduct investigations for guests who are visiting specifically to hunt for ghosts. In 2008 he was attending a friend's birthday celebration that is held every year at Lizzie Borden's. Besides his friend and her family, there were three other guests from California. The group was all gathered in the front parlor, listening to Matt recount the whole history of the house, the deaths, and the ghostly activity. The parlor, like all the rooms in the house, is furnished and decorated much as it would have been at the time of the murders, based on crime scene photographs. Moniz was sitting in a high-backed chair placed at a ninety-degree angle to a short sofa, where his friend was sitting. Between them, to the right of the chair, stood a small table. On this table, there was an eight-by-ten photograph of Second Street as it looked in the late nineteenth-century. The picture was under glass, in a heavy wooden frame and displayed on an ornate, metal stand. As Matt explained to his audience the changes that have occurred to the neighborhood over the years, he passed the photograph around to illustrate his point. When the picture was returned to him, he placed it carefully back on the metal stand. Before Moniz could finish his next sentence, the photograph and its stand lifted off the table. The heavy stand fell to the floor next to Matt's chair, but the picture held in the air for a brief instant before spinning out into the room. As the picture hit the floor, it rolled on the corners of its frame in a semi-circle before coming to a complete stop. Being the fearless paranormal investigator and scientist that he is, Moniz picked the picture and stand up off the floor, put them back together on the small table and enthusiastically requested, "Do it again!" With that, everyone, except his friend, fled the room in a slight panic.

The sounds of people walking around and talking on the second floor have been heard quite often. I have heard footsteps and banging coming from the upstairs during two visits to the house. Guests have told Lee-Ann and her staff that they were kept awake by the sound of someone walking around during the night. Another complaint is having their blankets pulled off or someone touching them while they were in bed. When I asked Lee-Ann to tell me about the scariest story told to her by an overnight guest, she answered, "I've had a few guests leave in the middle of the night, so I never do get their stories."

The attic on the third floor contains three comfortable guest rooms. All three of these rooms have had startling activity. Shortly after purchasing the property, Lee-Ann decided that she would spend the night on the third floor. She picked Bridget's room to sleep in. Bridget was the Bordens' live-in maid. She did not pass away in the house, but some paranormal investigators have suggested that she may haunt the house in periods of visitation, due to guilt felt over the murders. An old rocking chair sits in a corner of this room. Lee-Ann told me that she slept very well through the night, but when she woke up, the rocking chair was alongside the bed. It was as if someone had sat vigil over her while she slept.

The next room on the third floor is the Andrew Jennings room. It contains Lizzie Borden's own sewing machine. A banging sound has been traced to this room, and the apparent source is the cast-iron foot pedal banging against the sewing machine's wooden base. I once left a video camera running in the Hosea Knowlton room, which is next to the Jennings room. When I reviewed the video the next day, I found that the microphone had recorded a loud "thump, thump, thump" sound. When Matt Moniz listened to the recording, he smiled and said, "I've heard that sound before. It's Lizzie's sewing machine in the next room." Matt told me he traced the thumping sound one night to the Andrew Jennings room and saw the pedal fall against the wood as he entered the room.

The other strange thing I found on my video recording was the video itself. I had set my camera on a wooden chest in a corner of the Hosea Knowlton room. I picked this spot because Moniz and the paranormal group, Whaling City Ghosts, had placed a video camera in the very same spot on a previous investigation and it moved twice. The second time it moved, there were witnesses in the room looking directly at the camera. No one was near it. The video camera moved seemingly by invisible hands. My video camera didn't physically move, but the video image kept shifting around. The manufacturers of the camera told me over the phone that they could give me no explanation for how this could happen.

Spotlight On: Anawan Rock
Rehoboth, Massachusetts

Rehoboth, Massachusetts has been called the commonwealth's most haunted town. There are six well-known sites that have produced numerous reports of apparitions, strange lights, and disembodied voices. The Hornbine School, an historic, one-room schoolhouse located at the intersection of Hornbine Road and Baker Street is said to be haunted by the spirits of its former students and their teacher. On Reed Street, a mysterious man in black has been seen walking around the ruins of the Shad Pond Factory. When witnesses have gone to look for him, he disappeared without a trace.

The old Palmer River Burial Ground on Lake Street is haunted by the ghosts of a little boy and a Colonial soldier. During two separate, independent investigations, paranormal investigators Brianne Pouliot and Michael Markowicz both recorded electronic voice phenomenon (EVP) of a woman singing in the burial ground. My colleagues and I have dubbed this spirit "The Singing Lady of Palmer River."

The Shad Pond Factory

The Village Cemetery on Bay State Road contains no fewer than three specters. This graveyard has a ghost of a little boy that is seen dancing about the graves. There are also reports of a floating woman in white and a dark shade of a man in eighteenth-century garb that yells obscenities at women visiting the cemetery. This angry ghost has also been heard to cry out the name "Catherine" while positioned on his knees, pounding the ground with his fists.

On Route 44, near the Seekonk, Massachusetts, town line, a phantom referred to as "The Redheaded Hitchhiker" is said to walk the road late at night in the dead of winter. Dressed in denim jeans, work boots, and a flannel shirt, this redheaded ghost (some reports say he has a matching beard) harasses drivers by stepping out in front of their vehicles, forcing them to slam on the brakes. When the badly shaken driver looks for a body in the road, none is ever found. Stories claim that an awful, maniacal laughter, which seems to come from all directions, terrorizes the motorists.

Perhaps the most active haunted site in Rehoboth is a place called Anawan Rock. Located off of Route 44 East (about a half mile before the intersection with New Street), the rock is accessible by a short footpath that leads from a small, but well-marked parking lot. In 1676 the bloody "King Philip's War" came to an end. In June 1675, the English authorities in the Plymouth colony had pressured the Wamponoag sachem (chief), Metacomet, into a war he didn't want. His Christian name was Philip, and he defied King Charles II's rule over his people and their land. On August 12, 1676, Philip was betrayed and brutally executed at Mount Hope, Rhode Island. His last surviving general, Anawan, was hiding in Rehoboth at this rock formation, using the surrounding swamp as concealment while he and a small band of warriors debated their future. Captain Benjamin Church and a company of militia moved in through the swamp on August 28, taking Anawan and his men completely by surprise, and demanded their unconditional surrender. The Indians were then marched off in shackles to Plymouth, Massachusetts, and later executed. Their severed heads were displayed on pikes for all to see. For many years, people visiting this historic site have reported experiencing strange phenomena. Some claim they have seen phantom fires that gave off no heat, burned nothing, and then quickly faded away before their eyes like an image on film. Visitors have also reported the strong smell of burning wood as if they were standing right by a campfire that they could not see. It is believed these are the ghostly campfires of Anawan and his men.

Further astonishing encounters involve witnesses hearing voices speaking in what is believed to be a dialect of Algonquin, the language of the Wampanoags. Luann Jolly and Gabrielle Lawson, cofounders of the paranormal research group, Whaling City Ghosts, have recorded voices at Ananwan Rock speaking Wampanoag words meaning "friend" and "kinsmen." They also captured a voice speaking in English. One cold night in February, as the two ladies were approaching the rock from the parking lot, Luann reminded Gabrielle to be very careful and avoid injury in the dark. At that moment, their audio recorder captured a voice saying, "Here we go." When I heard this audio clip, I couldn't help but wonder if this was the trapped spirit of a militiaman, moving in on Ananwan and his men for all eternity.

That very same evening, Gabrielle Lawson videotaped balls of light moving past her while she was standing at the top of the rock. There was no wind that night and the weather was dry and cold. Whatever the orbs were, they could not have been snowflakes, and they certainly were not flying insects. The big shock of that night came towards the end of their investigation when Luann Jolly saw the figure of a man standing only a few feet away from her. Luann told me she only saw him briefly, but there was enough ambient light to make out the detail of his garments. She is certain the figure was an American Indian. Even though she cannot prove it, Luann's gut feeling tells her that it was Anawan's ghost.

On the evening of August 31, 2008, Matt Moniz of Spooky Southcoast Radio and I conducted our own investigation of Ananwan Rock. The first strange thing that occurred that night was a ball of light I saw hovering in the air behind the rock. It disappeared as soon as my mind acknowledged that it was there. I said nothing to Matt. A few minutes later, Matt saw the same floating orb himself. I asked him where he saw it and he pointed his flashlight beam to the exact same spot as my sighting.

Then Matt asked me to stand next to him and look out into the swamp. I saw nothing at first, but then I was astounded by the unmistakable sight of firelight flickering on the underside of the forest canopy. The light was fleeting, but anyone who has sat around a campfire knows what firelight looks like when it illuminates the underside of the leaves on the trees above. There was no visible light source that could have created this effect. We kept an eye out for it throughout the night, but never saw the firelight again.

The third thing that happened on our vigil really shook us up. Matt and I were standing only a few feet apart with our backs to one another. That August night was quite warm and there was no breeze to speak of. All of a sudden, the air between us became as cold as ice. It felt like someone had walked right between us, turning our skin into gooseflesh. Later Matt and I laughed as we recalled the looks on our faces at the very moment we turned around to face each other, not knowing what we were going to see.

Spotlight On:
The Freetown State Forest
Freetown, Massachusetts

The Freetown State Forest is a place well steeped in legends about devil-worshipping cults, gangster slayings, zombies, supernatural beings, and ghosts. My good friend Christopher Balzano has extensively researched the dark tales of the Freetown area and the state forest itself. On an afternoon in the spring of 2008, I met with Christopher at the forest's main entrance, and he gave me a guided tour of the most haunted places there. We were also there to meet up with Ron Kolek and members of his New England Ghost Project team for an investigation that night.

The first place Christopher brought to my attention was a spot called Profile Rock, located right off of Slab Bridge Road. The rock has a natural formation in the shape of the profile of a man's face. It is said that the local Wampanoags believed it resembled their great sachem, Massasoit. His son, Metacomet, would go there often to meditate and commune with his late father's spirit. Many hikers and mountain bikers use the paths around this part of the forest, and Christopher Balzano has interviewed some who have seen the ghost of a Native American on top of the rock.

From there, we drove to an area called the Reservation, located near the entrance of State Forest Road. On the way there, Christopher pointed out Copicut Road to me. He said that there are stories about a mad trucker who appears out of nowhere and hassles people driving along the road. This crazed phantom pulls up close to their car's rear bumper, honking his horn and flashing his lights as if he is in a desperate hurry. The mad trucker then disappears without a trace.

We turned onto State Forest Road (off of Bell Rock Road) and parked at a small, dirt lot. The Reservation is an area set aside for the

Wampanoags to hold their yearly meetings and spiritual powwows. Christopher has talked to people from all walks of life that have seen ghosts in and around the vicinity of the Reservation. One common thread in all their tales was that the witnesses did not feel threatened by any of these spirits.

A middle-aged couple very interested in Native American history and customs visited the Reservation in the summer of 2000. When they got out of their car, they heard the sound of drums coming from the forest where the Wampanoags hold their meetings. The couple assumed that there was a powwow in progress and decided to walk into the woods in the direction of the drums. They saw no one as they approached the meeting area. What they saw instead were five human sized columns of what looked like smoke or storm clouds, positioned motionless in the corner of the covered picnic pavilion. Even though they felt privileged to see such a sight, they thought it best to leave quietly.

Christopher spoke to a young woman who would sometimes go to the Reservation to pray, meditate, and practice Wicca. One afternoon while assembling an altar out of branches and other natural materials, she felt the sensation of being watched. When this feeling became too much for her, she went through the procedures needed to properly close down her altar. As soon as the young woman finished and started to leave, she caught sight of a teenaged boy skipping silently over the grass. He was wearing only a pair of pants; but stranger still, he was glowing a light green color. The strange boy stopped, looked right at her, and smiled. He then turned away and faded into thin air.

Before heading to our next haunted destination, The Assonet Ledge, Ron Kolek and members of his paranormal group arrived and assembled at the Reservation. They were hoping to capture evidence of the supernatural creatures that are said to inhabit the forest. The Wampanoags call them Puckwudgies. They are troll-like beasties that use balls of light called Tei-Pai-Wankas to lure unsuspecting victims to their doom. Ron and his team chose to walk through the forest under the light of the full moon while Christopher and I decided to take my four-by-four to the Assonet Ledge and meet them there.

The Assonet Ledge is an old, disused quarry located deep in the forest at the end of State Forest Road. The New England Ghost Project team was using a GPS unit to find the ledge as they walked along deer trails that paralleled the dirt road on which Christopher and I drove. Our two parties stayed in touch with hand-held radios. Shortly after Christopher and I arrived at the base of the quarry we tried to radio Ron's party. What we got back over the radio was something about their psychic, Maureen Wood, being attacked by an elemental.

While we waited for them to arrive at the old quarry, Christopher told me about the ghost that is often seen standing at the top of the Assonet Ledge. Known as "The Lady of the Ledge," this sad female ghost is thought to be a suicide victim who jumped to her death with a broken heart. Though this cannot be confirmed, there are many known suicides and accidental deaths at the Assonet Ledge. In the early 1990s, our friend Matt Moniz saw this ghost and thought she was a real, flesh-and-blood person. Matt had arrived at the top of the quarry right before sunset to do some stargazing with a few friends of his. As he walked out on the ledge, he noticed a woman in a white dress standing only a few yards off to his left. Matt turned around and told his friends that they weren't alone, and when he turned back, the woman was gone. There was no sound of a splash from the deep pool below, and the water was as smooth as glass when Matt looked over the edge. His friends stared at him for a moment and then explained that he had just seen "The Lady of The Ledge."

When the New England Ghost Project finally arrived at the base of the Assonet Ledge, they told Christopher and me about the encounter they had in the forest. Their psychic, Maureen, had sensed an evil presence stalking them through the woods. When they activated their thermal imager and pointed it in the direction Maureen instructed them to, the imager's screen showed a strange distortion hovering a few feet away. Maureen suddenly fell down and began to cry out as she rolled around on the ground. The team got on the ground with her and encouraged Maureen to fight whatever was attacking her. This worked and all went quiet. When they looked for the creepy distortion again with the thermal imager, they could not find it. The member of their team who was operating the imager is a professional firefighter who has been fully trained in the use of the sophisticated device. He told me he has never seen anything like that distortion before.

As we were all about to call it a night, it happened again. Maureen Wood started to behave strangely. She threw off her handbag and began growling with a twisted look on her face. She

The Lady of The Ledge haunts the old Assonet quarry.

almost backed into the quarry pool. Because we were standing at the bottom of the ledge, the fall wouldn't have been much, but the water is very deep. She and anyone else who may have jumped in to pull her out could have drowned. Ron and Christopher had to tackle Maureen and take her to the ground to stop her from going into the water. As they held her down, calling her back from whatever force was attacking her, Ron dislocated one of his fingers. While all this was happening, I was shooting video in infrared. As I watched the whole event unfold through the camera's view screen, I noticed a strange little light appear behind the group as they huddled around Maureen on the ground. The light lasted for thirteen seconds before it disappeared. I walked right up to the spot where the point of light was, and I found nothing on the ground, such as broken glass, that could account for what I'd seen.

We packed all of the team's equipment into my vehicle, and I drove Ron Kolek, Maureen Wood, and another female member of their team back to the Reservation. Christopher Balzano and the other three male members of Ron's expedition walked back along the road under the light of the full moon. When Christopher and his party reached the parking lot, they reported another sighting of the weird distortion. As they were walking along State Forest Road, the three members of Ron's team estimated that they were not too far from the area where they had seen the distortion earlier that night. Even though they weren't in exactly the same spot, they felt it was worth a shot. They turned on the thermal imager and began scanning the forest. As they scanned the forest, the distortion reappeared. As before, the anomaly started off as a head-sized blob, but grew rapidly. As it grew, it began to move towards them. Christopher told me later that he could not explain what he had seen on the thermal imager's screen. He only had a few seconds to observe the distortion because the three brave members of the New England Ghost Project took off running down the road with the imager in hand. In the world of ghosthunting, we call a panicked reaction like this "pulling a Scooby-Doo."

CHAPTER 4

USS *Salem*

QUINCY, MASSACHUSETTS

AFTER 102 YEARS OF SHIPBUILDING HISTORY, the Fore River shipbuilding facility in Quincy, Massachusetts, was closed down in 1986. In 1993, thanks to the dedicated efforts of local officials and volunteers, the location was reopened as the United States Naval Shipbuilding Museum. It was decided that the proper centerpiece for this heritage site should be a naval vessel that was actually built and laid down at the old shipyard. Through negotiations with the United States Navy, the museum was able to obtain the USS *Salem* (CA-139) out of Philadelphia where it had been in "mothballs" for thirty-five years. The *Salem* finally returned home to Quincy, Massachusetts, on October 30, 1994. On May 14, 1995 (the forty-sixth anniversary of her origi-

nal commissioning), the USS *Salem* was re-commissioned as a member of the Historic Naval Ships Association.

The Des Moines class heavy cruiser was found in remarkably good condition, even though the ship's interior should have been badly corroded from all the years it sat idle. Years ago, budget cuts forced the U.S. Navy to order the shutdown of all the dehumidification systems that were protecting their deactivated ships from rusting away while in storage. It is believed that somewhere along the chain of command, someone may have disregarded those orders and allowed the dehumidifiers on the *Salem* to continue running, perhaps out of love for the old lady. This action (or inaction) protected the ship from years of damaging moisture. It has been estimated that this heavy cruiser, in her present condition, could be made seaworthy and combat-ready in only eight months. This is a pretty amazing fact, especially when one takes into consideration that the *Salem* was launched in 1947.

At seven hundred feet in length and seventy-seven feet at her beam, the *Salem* is quite an intimidating battlewagon. Armed with nine eight-inch guns, twelve five-inch guns, and eighteen three-inch guns, this heavy battle cruiser once packed a powerful punch. However, in its ten years of service, the *Salem* never fired a shot in anger. During the Cold War, the USS *Salem* played more of a diplomatic role while operating as flagship for the Second Fleet in the Atlantic and for the Sixth Fleet in the Mediterranean.

She was the first ship to respond to the massive earthquake that devastated the Ionian Islands off Greece in 1953. The ship's crew helped rescue civilians from the terrible destruction and evacuated the injured to the *Salem* for emergency treatment. Unfortunately, many of those people were too badly hurt and they passed away while onboard. It is believed that some of the ghosts haunting the vessel are lost souls from that horrible tragedy in Greece.

The ship's wardroom served as the officer's mess and conference room. There has been a great deal of paranormal activity experienced in this area of the ship.

I was invited to take part in a paranormal investigation of the USS *Salem* by two colleagues of mine, Kathy Caslin and Eric LaVoie. Don DeCristofaro, a former sailor, gave us a tour of the ship. Don is currently serving as a tour guide for the USS *Salem* and has come to accept the ghosts that haunt the ship's passageways and cabins. I asked Don about the victims who died aboard the *Salem* during the humanitarian mission in Greece and whether he thought their deaths might be a source of the paranormal activity that's been reported throughout the ship since it opened as a museum. Don replied by saying, "The women and children who are entities aboard the ship, it's only natural to assume they are Greek civilians. I don't know this for a fact, but I would be surprised if there was a ship in the history of the United States Navy that saw no action, but saw as much death as the Salem."

On a much brighter note, there were over twenty successful births delivered by the ship's medical staff. Sadly though, there were also a number of mothers and babies lost during childbirth due to the trauma they had suffered in the earth-quake. The ship's surgery is felt by some to be haunted by the spirits of those women and their infants who died on the operating table. People have reported hearing female voices coming from inside the surgery, and some claimed to have seen a dark form, like a person's shadow, moving around in the room's confined space.

An incident that took place in the ship's wardroom during a previous investigation also appears to support the belief that there are spirits of women haunting the *Salem*. In the summer of 2010, Don DeCristafaro was assisting a ghosthunting group whose founders are also husband and wife. The team had decided to use the wardroom as their base of operations for the night, despite the fact that one of the two psychics who works with them had said she felt "something strange" about the room. Perhaps they should have listened to her psychic intuition because as Don said, "Things got so bad in here we had to turn on all the lights and call the husband on the radio to come get his wife because she kinda' puddled."

What Don meant by "bad" was that the atmosphere in the room got very heavy. A short while after the husband had left with the other half of their group to investigate the lower decks, the wardroom became very active with sound and movement. Don told me, "At one point, the psychic called out, 'where are you?,' because it seemed like there were things in every corner of the room."

There was a loud noise from the far side of the room, and when the team looked to see what had caused the racket, they found a chair tipped over on its side. Don and the four investigators then withdrew from the wardroom and stepped out into the passageway. As they stood close together, trying to take in what was happening, they heard a woman let out a loud moan. Don said, "It was so loud that all five of us turned and said, 'what the hell was that!'" The ghosthunters' audio recorder captured the mournful wail, making it hard to dismiss as over-active imaginations and rattled nerves.

This is not the only unexplainable sound that Don has heard on the ship. In fact, his first ghostly encounter on the *Salem* was the unmistakable sound of a barking dog. Don and a co-worker named Katy were the only two people onboard as they went about closing the museum down for the night. Katy waited for Don on an upper deck as he climbed up the steep ladder from the ship's combat information center (CIC), which is located in the bowels of the ship. The CIC is not featured on public tours because it is accessed via a long ladder with steel rungs. When Don reached the top of the ladder, he looked at Katy, wondering if she could hear what he was hearing: a dog barking down below in CIC. By the time he climbed back down into the ship's belly, the barking had stopped and there was no dog to be found. Don informed me that many of the Greek refugees brought their pets with them when they were evacuated to the *Salem*.

Another active area that has a strong connection to the deaths of the Greek civilians is located below one of the crew's berthing quarters and is referred to as the "butter room." It is called this because it is a walk-in refrigerator where the ship's supply of eggs and butter were stored. This cold storage room made an ideal place to store the bodies of the civilian casualties who passed away while onboard. Don told me that he has never seen or heard anything in the butter room himself, but others have reported hearing voices and felt very uneasy while investigating this onetime morgue.

There are reasons to believe that some of the paranormal activity aboard ship is related to the spirits of sailors. One possible ghost could be a sailor who fell to his death in the ship's elevator shaft while working to prepare the deactivated ship for storage. A possible psychic link that may also be allowing the spirits of other sailors to haunt the ship is the permanent display of items from the *Salem*'s sister ship, the USS *Newport News*

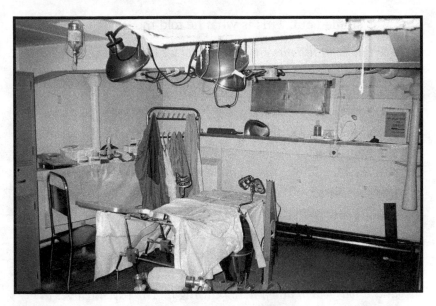

The ship's surgery. People have reported seeing shadowy figures moving about in this confined space. Female voices have also been heard here.

(CA-148). This museum-within-a-museum is a heartfelt tribute to the *Newport News's* service to our country and her tragic loss of twenty crewmen during the Viet Nam conflict. There is a theory in paranormal research that suggests that objects can hold psychic energy from people who had a strong connection to that item while they were still alive.

A male figure has been seen a number of times in the chief petty officers' mess. People have caught only fleeting glimpses of this man, so there are no clues as to his identity. Shadowy figures have also been sighted in the crew's mess. Two unrelated psychic investigators picked up on a male entity in the crew's mess. Both psychics described the entity as being a verbally abusive seaman who doesn't want people to be in that area of the ship. When Don was first told this, he openly challenged the aggressive spirit with the fact that he, Don, was a sailor too and he wasn't afraid of anyone. Nothing happened, so he left it at that. However, a few months later, when the second psychic sensed this rude spirit,

Don was singled out. This is what he told me:

> *I was here in the mess with a group; we had been in here for*
> *a little while when their psychic said, "He's here now and he's*
> *laughing at us. He thinks we're the funniest thing ever." And*
> *then she said, "He hates you." And I said, "Me?" She said,*
> *"Yeah, he says you think you're tougher than him, and he's*
> *telling me to get you out of here." So, I'm just standing there,*
> *and then she says to me, "You're ready to go, aren't you? You*
> *look real pissed off." I didn't know what she was talking about*
> *until I realized that my hand was bleeding in one place from*
> *me clenching my fist. Then she says, "Oh yeah, you're both*
> *ready for a fight and you don't even know it." Now, of course,*
> *I'm baffled. Then all of a sudden, my back was freezing cold,*
> *and it was warm down here that night. The psychic looks at*
> *me and says, "Don, he's right on your back; he is right on*
> *you." Then it stopped. The cold went away, and it was all*
> *over—just like that. That was the night I walked away from*
> *here thinking this is a creepy place.*

The USS *Salem* does appear to have one friendly ghost. His name was John Schaffer, and he was a native of Quincy, Massachusetts, who served onboard the *Salem* as a warrant officer while the ship was on active duty. When the *Salem* was brought back to the Fore River facility, John volunteered to help with the restoration work. He even lived on the ship and had his own cabin. He also died on the ship. Schaffer suffered a heart attack while in the anchor windlass room, which is the most forward area of the ship and contains the machinery for raising and lowering the ship's anchors. Don told me that he has never encountered John Schaffer himself, but the museum's director, Michael Condon, has talked with people on the quarter deck as they were leaving the ship who have commented on how helpful John was with answering their questions. Don said, "Mike's a pretty straight up guy, so I tend to believe what he tells me."

CHAPTER 5

Stone's Public House
ASHLAND, MASSACHUSETTS

Stone's Public House is a splendid place for good food, live music, and ghost stories.

IN 1831 CAPTAIN JOHN STONE obtained insider information that the Boston and Worcester Railroad would be running a line right through his property in the town of Ashland (then, Hopkinton), Massachusetts. John Stone was no fool; he knew there was a profit to be made from the many travelers who would soon be arriving in the town. He began construction of a hotel in 1832 and positioned the building close to where he was told the new train station would stand. The hotel was named the Railroad House, and it was completed just in time for the opening of the railway line on September 20, 1834. More than three hundred people turned out that day for the fanfare. Governor John Davis and former Governor Levi Lincoln, both addressed the crowd. Some accounts say Daniel Webster was also in attendance.

One of the local papers at the time, the *Farmers Gazette*, reported that there were stagecoaches running from the Railroad House to Worcester and Unionville. The paper also noted that conveyances could be obtained at Stone's hotel for visitors wanting to travel locally. It seemed that Captain Stone had all his moneymaking angles well thought out. One thing he didn't plan correctly, however, was the proximity of the Railroad House to the train tracks. Stone started building the hotel without a clear understanding of where the railroad company was going to lay the tracks. This miscalculation on his part placed the hotel so close to the railway line that passing locomotives would nearly rattle the guests out of their beds.

John Stone turned management of the hotel over to his son, Napoleon Bonaparte Stone, only a year after the business opened. There is a legend about why Stone had his son take over the daily operations of the business. The tale claims that Captain Stone had a heated argument with a traveling salesman from New York over a game of cards. Angry words grew into violence, and supposedly Stone killed the man by striking a blow to the head with the butt of a pistol. Stone supposedly buried the salesman's body in the dirt-floor cellar. Some believe Stone stayed away from the hotel because he was afraid of the murdered man's ghost. However, no one really knows if the salesman ever did haunt the place.

A man named William A. Scott bought the hotel in 1859 and renamed it W. A. Scott and Sons Livery and Hotel. He owned the hotel and stables until 1904. During Scott's time as the proprietor, he and his family went through a lot of pain and sorrow.

This heartache could be relevant to the haunting at Stone's Public House, but more on that later.

The ghost stories didn't become public knowledge until about 1976 when a man named Leonard "Cappy" Fournier bought the property. The building was in a bad state by then and needed much repair and restoration. Anyone familiar with tales of haunted places knows that ghostly activity seems to pick up when an old building undergoes reconstruction. Strange things began to happen shortly after Fournier started the restoration work. He and the contractors would lock the place up at the end of the day and return the next morning to find the doors unlocked and wide open. They would hear footsteps, doors slamming, and faucets would turn on by themselves. A psychic named Raffaele Bibbo visited the restaurant in the mid-1980s and felt the chief spirit haunting the building was John Stone himself, racked with guilt over the murder he had committed those many years before. The ghost most associated with Stone's is that of a little girl who has been seen and heard many times throughout the building by guests and employees.

There have been a few sightings of this sad little girl in the downstairs dining room, but most witnesses have reported seeing her looking out at them from the second floor and attic windows. In October of 2010, I spoke to the general manager of Stone's Public House, Ben Stoetzel. Ben started working at Stone's as a bartender in 2006 and had not heard anything about the ghost until his first night working at the bar.

Appropriately enough, it was Halloween night. Nothing strange occurred that evening, but one afternoon in the winter of 2008 left Ben with little doubt that there was something to the stories he had been told by his fellow employees and regular customers. Stoetzel came in on a Monday to take inventory of the bar's stock. The business was closed and he had brought along his one-and-a-half year old daughter for company. They

This young girl's apron was found in the attic. Some believe there is a connection between this article of clothing and the ghost of Mary Jane Smith.

were the only two people in the building; all the doors were locked and the place was very still. As Ben stood behind the bar with his clipboard, checking off what was in stock, he kept a close eye on his little girl, who was standing at the front of the bar. Ben said, "She let out a little, high-pitched giggle for no reason and almost instantly I heard a very similar giggle that to my hearing came from the complete opposite side of the room. My head jerked around, I looked back at my daughter and she was as happy as a clam. So I just went check, check, check, check on my clipboard and thought, 'OK, work's done for the day,' and we left."

Ghost stories at Stone's are not the topic of conversation in the Stoetzel's home. When Ben is home he likes to concentrate on his family and leave the job behind. It is because of this that

Ben is sure he has never put the notion of phantoms from his workplace in his young daughter's impressionable mind. But one year after hearing the unexplainable giggle in the bar, his daughter brought up another afternoon she had visited Stone's with her dad. The business had three big repair jobs being taken care of on a Monday while the place was closed. Ben and an assistant manager, Gregg, had stopped by to make sure that the three work crews were on schedule and everything was going as planned. Both men had brought along their daughters and had left them in the care of one of the employees, Erica. The three of them remained in the bar and out of the way while Ben and the Gregg checked on the progress of the work crews.

A few weeks later, Ben's daughter brought up that afternoon and when he was sure that they were both referring to the same day, she told him all about "playing with Bella (Gregg's daughter) and her friends." When Ben reminded her that it was only Erica and Bella with her that day, she insisted that there were several other children with them in the bar. He asked her to describe the children, but she could only remember one of them in detail. His daughter said there was a girl, a little taller than her, in a black dress with black hair. "It creeped me right out and gave me gooseflesh," said Ben. A few months later, Stoetzel overheard a ghosthunter give a group of guests the accepted description of the little girl's ghost. It exactly matched what Ben's daughter had told him.

On one of my visits to Stone's Public House, I met with a local researcher, David Francis. David has been investigating the bar and restaurant for more than four years and has done a terrific job piecing together the building's past. A colleague of his, David Retalic, along with Cliff Wilson of the Ashland Historic Commission, found a death register from 1862 which records the death of a Mary Jane Smith. A report from the Boston and Worcester Railroad states, "June 11—Mary Jane Smith, eleven years old, disregarded the warning of the flagman at Ashland, attempted to cross the track directly in front of a passing train, was run over and instantly killed." Since the days of Cappy Fournier, people have been saying that the little girl who haunts the building was struck by a train and her body was brought inside the hotel. A young girl's apron, matching the same time period, was found in the attic several years ago. Some believe it may have belonged to Mary Jane Smith, though there is no evidence of this. The apron has since been framed under glass and is displayed on the second floor.

The death of Mary Jane Smith could explain the identity of the restaurant's best-known ghost, but what of the "other" children? David Francis told me that on two separate occasions, children were seen at the windows on the second floor by customers eating outside on the patio. A concerned lady reported to one of the waitresses that she had seen a little girl hanging out of one of the upstairs windows. When the waitress went out on the patio to see for herself, there was no girl at the window. The waitress then explained that those rooms are used for storage only and no one could have been up there. She also pointed out to the customer that the window the child was hanging out of was in fact closed. Not too long after that sighting, another customer complained about seeing children, looking very distressed, standing at the windows above the patio. David Francis has no theories as to who these little ghosts are or why they would be haunting an old railway inn.

David Francis has compiled an extensive timeline of the building's long history. It was his research that uncovered the tragic events that plagued the former owner, William A. Scott. In the forty-five years Scott owned the hotel he lost two of his sons, Lawrence and Edward, to cirrhosis of the liver and a third, George, to madness. Before George was committed to the Worcester Lunatic Asylum, he attacked two people in the hotel.

His father beat him with a cane in order to stop the assault.

In 1889, a fire in the stables killed nine horses and damaged the hotel. It is said the fire devastated Scott emotionally. In 1899, W. A. Scott attempted suicide with a revolver. He lost his wife, Caroline, two years later. She had suffered for many months from kidney disease before finally passing away. It is possible that the pain and torment of the Scott family has tainted the building psychically.

I was given a compact disc containing eighteen very impressive examples of EVP that were recorded by David Francis and his fellow investigators at Stone's over a four-year period. Three of the EVPs suggest that members of the Scott family may still linger within the walls of the old building. A woman's voice was captured twice on the third floor. Her first comment was, "You're all drunk." The second time she is heard saying, "I see that you're all drunk." This could be Mrs. Scott addressing her sons Lawrence and Edward. The third EVP was recorded on the second floor as an electromagnetic field meter sounded a reaction. It is a male voice saying the name, "Lawrence."

In my conversation with Ben Stoetzel, he made mention of the atmosphere at Stone's Public House. He has been in the restaurant-and-bar industry for more than sixteen years and has worked in ten different locations. Ben told me, "I have never seen a place that brings out such a heightened sense of emotion like this place does. This place is a magnet for unusual behavior. I think that whatever has happened here in the 176-plus years has left some kind of impression on the physical structure that just changes the way people act."

CHAPTER 6

The Groton Inn

THIS PROPERTY WAS DESTROYED BY FIRE IN AUGUST 2011.

THE GROTON INN is one of the oldest taverns in New England. The original structure was a small family dwelling (half-house) built around 1723 by a man named Samuel Parker. That house was enlarged in 1761 when it became the residence of the Reverend Samuel Dana. He lived there until 1775. The reverend's loyalist leanings made him very unpopular, and he was forced to leave his ministry. The next person to own the property was Captain Jonathan Keep. He opened the building as a stagecoach tavern in 1780 and called it Cap'n Keep's Tavernstand.

The town's third meetinghouse, which was first erected in 1714, was brought to Captain Keep's property in the early 1790s and joined to the east side of the inn. A third building, the former Richardson's Tavern, was later attached to the inn's north side in 1840. That structure was originally built in 1678 and once served the town as a garrison house. The inn's front porch was also added during the renovations of 1840. The end result of this harmonious conglomeration is a handsome tavern, which is considered by many to be the central point of Groton's historic district.

There are some other noteworthy facts about the Groton Inn's long history. From 1797 to 1847, the inn was used as the meeting place for the St. Paul's Masonic Lodge. Paul Revere was the Grand Master who performed the lodge's installation ceremonies. It has been recognized as America's oldest Masonic meeting place. The inn was a stop on the Underground Railway as well. Runaway slaves were moved through an underground tunnel that once ran from beneath a former outbuilding to a house on the grounds of the neighboring Lawrence Academy. The number of historic figures who have stayed here is rather impressive too. Henry Wadsworth Longfellow, Andrew Carnegie, and President Ulysses S. Grant are only a few of the prominent names from the Groton Inn's register. The inn was purchased in 1977 by its current owner, George Pergantis. The old building was showing its age, and a substantial overhaul was needed to put things right. Mr. Pergantis saw to it personally that all the necessary renovations were carried out with absolute regard for the inn's historic character. It was during this process of renewal that the owner and his staff heard their very first ghost story at the inn.

A builder named Andy had been staying at the inn while working with George Pergantis on the building's restoration. Late one night, he woke up suddenly and saw a Colonial soldier sitting in a chair at the foot of the bed. Andy was not sure if he was dreaming, so he rubbed his eyes and took a second look.

The soldier was still sitting in the chair. As soon as Andy real-ized that he was awake and not dreaming, he demanded that the soldier explain himself. The soldier just smiled, tipped his cap, and vanished without a trace.

When the work was completed, the Old Groton Inn reopened its doors on December 15, 1990. Gloria Lammi is a good friend of the owner and has been one of the inn's managers for more than thirty years. She told me that her first encounter with para-normal activity in the building happened about two weeks after reopening. Gloria received a phone call one morning from the day cook, Patty, informing her that there were some strange and upsetting things happening at the inn. Patty and a waitress were so frightened by what had been going on that morning that they ran across the street and used a pay phone to call Gloria. They wanted her to come right away.

As soon as Gloria arrived she could see how distressed the women were. Since there were no guests staying at the inn, she ushered the two employees into the reception area and asked them to explain what had happened. Patty said when she came in early that morning she had switched the lights on in the tav-ern and then went into the kitchen to light the gas ovens. A few minutes later, Patty went back into the tavern and found all the lights off, the bar sinks were running and the telephone on the bar was off the hook. She turned the lights back on, shut the sinks off, and hung the phone back up. The doors to the building were locked. When Patty returned to the kitchen, she discovered the ovens were now off and someone had wrapped the support columns with plastic food wrap. The day waitress arrived soon afterwards, and Patty told her what had been going on. Shortly after that, the coffee maker went on by itself. That's when they ran across the street and called Gloria.

While Gloria was standing at the reception desk, trying her best to take in what the cook and waitress had just told her, a

The doorway where the dark shadow figure was seen by the inn's bartender.

light on the telephone lit up indicating that someone was using the telephone in the tavern. She told the two women to run to the bar and see who was there. Gloria said, "I stayed there (at the reception desk) and held the phone up to my ear. It was crackling terribly, a funny crackling noise, loud. Then it stopped abruptly and I heard Patty say, 'Look, it's off the hook again.' There couldn't have been anyone there playing a prank; they would have been caught."

The activity continued throughout the rest of the day and evening. A basket of potpourri was spilled out all over the ladies room and the toilet paper roll was completely unraveled. The bed in room number one was discovered with its blankets and sheets messed up. The maid remade the bed, and Gloria told her to make sure that the door was locked when she was done. The maid went back to the room about fifteen minutes later, unlocked the door, and found the bed pulled apart again.

That very same evening, a waitress found the water glasses and napkins from one of the dining room tables sitting on the floor as if someone had placed them there. She set them back on the table and reported it to Gloria. When the waitress went back and found the water glasses back on the floor, Gloria told her to leave them alone. At the end of the night, the glasses were found back on the table, stacked like a pyramid.

The dining room in which these water glasses moved about is referred to as the "Grandma Moses Room" because it is decorated with prints by the well-known American folk artist. On two separate occasions, two individual waitresses have caught sight of an old woman seated at a table in this room. When they went back to see if she had been waited on, the old woman was nowhere to be found. Gloria Lammi told me that she has a cousin who is gifted with second sight. During a conversation over the phone, her cousin informed Gloria that there is a ghost of an old woman haunting one of the dining rooms, and the ghost looks like Grandma Moses.

There have been other reports of the ghostly soldier since the inn reopened in 1990. In fact, one patron commented that her own father saw the soldier many years ago when the Groton Inn was under different management. A more recent sighting took place in the main dining room by a customer who was having dinner with his wife. While eating his meal, the man suddenly felt the uncomfortable sensation of being watched. Unnerved by this feeling, he turned around and was shocked to see the translucent figure of a Colonial soldier standing by the fireplace. The couple had no prior knowledge of the Groton Inn's haunted reputation. It is interesting to note that Gloria Lammi's psychic cousin and Laurie Cabot (the official witch of Salem, Massachusetts) both said they sensed a Colonial soldier haunting the inn.

I asked the bartender, Vicky-Jean, if she had ever experienced anything unusual during her time at the inn. Vicky-Jean told me she had seen something weird only a few weeks before my visit. The event took place around eight-thirty at night in the tavern. She was standing behind the bar chatting with one of her regular customers, a man named Douglas. While listening to Douglas, she became aware of a dark shape standing in the doorway to the dining room area. Vicky-Jean said, "It was like a silhouette of a very heavyset man. His nose was extremely big, and you could see his hair was curled, and maybe he was wearing a little cap. I turned my head away and looked again to make sure I was actually seeing this—and I was. It was still there." All she could say to Douglas was, "Shadow!" Before he could turn to see it, the shadowy form vanished in an instant.

Victoria Carson has been an employee at the Groton Inn for more than ten years and currently oversees the inn's guestrooms. Victoria has heard some very strange stories about certain rooms from guests and employees. She herself has heard the sound of someone walking around in room seven, which is right above her office, when she knows the room is vacant. Noises like that have to be investigated for security reasons. The room is always found locked with no signs of anyone having been in there. Victoria had something very startling happen to her when she stayed overnight in room nine. While lying in bed, trying to fall asleep, she felt a strange urge to look towards the door to the room. As soon as she did, the door inexplicably flew wide open. Victoria said, "There was no one there. I was so scared, I couldn't scream. I hid under the covers until I was able to fall asleep!"

Room ten is considered to be the most active of all the guestrooms. Victoria Carson's son wanted to stay overnight at the inn to see if anything spooky would happen. Victoria told me that her son was treating the whole adventure as a joke. It was weeks before he could bring himself to talk to his mother about what he saw that night. He told her that as he was approaching rooms nine and ten, he noticed that the door to room ten was wide open and a woman was sitting on the bed. He averted his eyes out of politeness as he unlocked the door to room nine. After a couple of seconds it occurred to him that no one was supposed to be staying at the inn that night. When he looked back into room ten, the lady was gone. Victoria's son then began to take it all in and realized that the woman had been wearing an old fashioned dress and bonnet. Others have reported seeing this woman as well.

A colleague of mine, Kathy Caslin, has been investigating the Groton Inn for some time now and has done a remarkable job in researching the building's history. She believes the female spirits that haunt the inn are the Hoar sisters. The Hoar family owned and operated the inn from 1854 until the turn of the century. Kathy feels the sisters may still be looking after the family business which they were devoted to when they were alive. Perhaps the poltergeist activity is their way of keeping the inn's staff on their toes.

Kathy Caslin has had some very interesting moments at the Groton Inn. One time in particular was when she and her nephew, Ed Perry, spent a night in room ten in an attempt to capture evidence of paranormal activity. Ed fell asleep on the floor and Kathy had eventually done so on the bed. When dawn arrived, Kathy became aware of hands pushing her awake. As she opened her eyes, Kathy expected to see Ed standing over her because she knew he had to be at work early that morning. No one was standing by the bed and she could hear her nephew snoring on the floor. She got off the bed, woke Ed up and packed her equipment as fast as she could. She didn't say anything to Ed until they were driving away in her car.

Spotlight On: The Victorian
Gardner, Massachusetts

Gardner, Massachusetts, is referred to as "Chair City" because it has been a major center for furniture design and manufacturing since the early nineteenth century. One of the best-known residents from Gardner's past was the furniture magnate, Sylvester K. Pierce. In 1875 he built a splendid mansion for himself directly across the street from his factory on West Broadway. The original factory has long since been replaced, but his Victorian mansion remains as a splendid reminder of the Gilded Age.

The mansion, known locally as "The Victorian," contains twenty-six rooms, a large basement, and a turret that provides a fantastic view of the surrounding area. In its long history, many famous people have visited the mansion such as, President Calvin Coolidge, Norman Rockwell, and the actress Betty Davis. The billiard legend "Minnesota Fats" once played pool here on the third floor. A regular guest to the home in Pierce's day was P. T. Barnum, the founder of The Ringling Brothers and Barnum & Bailey Circus.

In the winter of 2008, Edwin and Lillian Gonzalez purchased the mansion with the desire to save and protect this beautiful, historic home. The Gonzalezes were told about the mansion's haunted reputation shortly after they had placed a bid on the property, but that didn't concern either of them because the couple didn't believe in ghosts. Their belief systems would start to change after they moved in during the spring of 2009.

On the very first day that Edwin and Lillian started moving their belongings into the house, they and their friends were taking a much-needed break in the dinning room. While eating pizza and chatting, they all heard a heavy dragging sound coming from right outside the room in the hallway by the front door. The sound was made by two heavy plant stands that had been brought in that day and placed temporarily in the hallway. They know the sound was made by the stands moving because they actually saw them shudder a few inches along the floor. The Gonzalezes thought this was strange, but shrugged it off.

One afternoon before they had finished moving in, Edwin arrived at the mansion to do some work on the old place. He was greeted by a neighbor who made a friendly comment about not knowing that Edwin and Lillian were parents. Edwin informed the neighbor that he and his wife had no children and then asked the man why he thought they did. The neighbor looked at Edwin in disbelief and explained that he had seen a little boy inside the house, running by the windows that face his home next door. The Gonzalezes learned later that this little boy is one of The Victorian's ghosts.

Once the couple settled in, the paranormal activity became even more noticeable. They began hearing knocking and tapping sounds, as well as footsteps on the main staircase. Their front doorbell sometimes rings when no one is there, and, as with the knockings, the sound repeats three times.

Early one morning, Edwin and Lillian were asleep in the master bedroom on the second floor when the front doorbell awakened them. They were expecting a male relative that morning, but it was too early in the morning for it to have been him. The doorbell rang two more times, and then within a matter of seconds, someone knocked loudly on their bedroom door. Edwin jumped out of bed and pulled the bedroom door open. No one was there or downstairs at the front door. A search of the mansion turned up nothing.

Their bedroom door also slammed shut on another occasion. The ghost believed to be responsible for the activity in the master bedroom was a man named Enos Saari. Saari lived at the Victorian during the mid-twentieth century when it served as a boardinghouse. The Gonzalezes' bedroom was once Saari's apartment. He died there April 10, 1963, in an accidental fire caused by the combination of cigarettes and moonshine. Before finding out about this man's unfortunate demise, Edwin saw a ghost that he now believes was that of Enos Saari.

Edwin was working late one night in his office, which is located on the mansion's second floor. As he sat at his desk, a man's face came around the right side of the computer monitor and stared directly at him. Shocked, Edwin toppled over in his chair. He jumped right up, prepared to deal with whoever the intruder was, but no one was there. This was the turning point for Edwin Gonzalez; he accepted the fact that he had bought a haunted house.

I first met Edwin only a few days after this encounter. While driving through the city of Gardner one afternoon in 2010, I decided to stop by The Victorian and ask the current owners if they had ever experienced anything unusual in the mansion. Edwin thought I was salesman when he answered the door, but after I introduced myself as a paranormal researcher, he was happy to talk with me about the house. He was amazed when I confirmed that The Victorian was considered by many to be one of the most haunted places in Massachusetts. The story of Enos Saari especially fascinated him.

Since my conversation with Edwin that afternoon, the Gonzalezes have looked deep into the history of the mansion. They have also invited several paranormal groups and psychics to conduct investigations of their home. Most of these groups have captured EVPs, and some have seen and heard things they could not explain. Edwin and Lillian both agree that the most amazing moment so far was when Ron Kolek and The New England Ghost Project used a shot of whiskey to entice a response from Enos Saari. As Kolek poured the glass, he asked Saari if he would like a shot of good whiskey. Everyone in the room heard a lustful voice reply, "Yeah!"

Spotlight On: The Victorian
(continued)

The psychic I work with, Pamela Patalano, hit upon the spirit of Enos Saari while she was in his old room. She said he had a scar on his face and used to make his own moonshine in the basement. Later, when we took her down into the basement, Pamela pointed to a spot and told us that was where he hid his alcohol still. A few months later, the Gonzalezes received a visit from Enos Saari's nephew, Paul. He confirmed everything Pamela Patalano had told us about his uncle. Edwin told me later that he could not get over the shocking resemblance between Paul Saari and the face he saw that night in his office. Edwin said, "The poor guy must have been wondering why I was staring at him the whole time he was here."

The Gonzalezes live with two Maltese dogs. Their dogs seem to watch and react to things that Edwin and Lillian can't see. There are also certain spots in the house the dogs will avoid. One day the couple was playing with their pets by throwing treats along the floor in the front hallway. The dogs would race to get the treats and then come back to do it again. Their dogs were having fun, so Edwin threw some more treats. The two excited dogs once again ran after them, but suddenly came to an abrupt stop in the same spot. The dogs stared as if someone was between them and their treats. The little dogs then turned around and ran back to Edwin and Lillian for protection. Sometime after this happened, a psychic informed them that one of their ghosts is a woman who hates having pets in the house.

In my most recent phone conversation with Edwin Gonzalez, he told me he has seen a shadowy figure of a man on the main staircase and a dark figure in the basement. The most recent story Edwin had to tell me involved the young son of his new neighbor. The boy's mother introduced herself to Edwin and asked him about "his son." When Edwin explained that he didn't have a son, the woman looked confused. She told Edwin that her own son had said there was a little boy next door who wanted to play with him, but he couldn't leave his house. When she asked which house, her son pointed to the Gonzalez home. Her son also added that the little boy wanted him to come to the second floor and play in the hallway. Not wanting to scare his new neighbor, Edwin played dumb and wished her a nice day.

The experience of living in a haunted house has changed the Gonzalezes' whole outlook on life and death. At the time of this writing, they are making plans to organize public tours and ghosthunts of their beautiful home. Check the Contact Information page in this book for more details.

CHAPTER 7

Houghton Mansion
NORTH ADAMS, MASSACHUSETTS

THE CITY OF NORTH ADAMS, Massachusetts, is situated within a valley in the midst of the beautiful Berkshire Mountains. The area was first settled in 1745, and by the start of the American Revolution there were already numerous water powered mills along the banks of the Hossic River. For three hundred years, this location produced businesses that manufactured everything from hats and shoes, to bricks and pig iron. North Adams was incorporated in 1875 and thrived as a mill town until the 1980s. Today the city is known as a center for recreation, tourism, and the Massachusetts Museum of Contemporary Art.

The art museum occupies the former sight of the Arnold Print Works. This once-prosperous textile company was the largest employer in North Adams. In 1874, a local businessman and philanthropist named Albert C. Houghton bought into the business to help save it from total collapse. The venture succeeded and the factory stayed in business until 1942. A. C. Houghton was also the city's first mayor. He was a true leader in the community and well respected. The Houghton family lived in a mansion located on Church Street, and as far as local historians can tell, they lived a happy and comfortable life; that is until August 1, 1914.

On that fateful summer day, A. C. Houghton, his daughter Mary, his niece Sybil and her husband, Dr. Robert Hutton, took a trip to Bennington, Vermont, in the family's new Pierce Arrow automobile. At the wheel of the vehicle was the Houghton's carriage driver and right-hand man, John Widders. While driving through Pownal, Vermont, Widders was forced to take evasive action to avoid hitting a team of horses that was stopped on the road. He lost control of the car and it left the dirt track, rolling violently down a steep embankment. John Widders, A. C. Houghton, and Dr. Hutton survived the crash with minor injuries, but Mrs. Hutton died at the scene. Mary Houghton succumbed to her injuries while on route to the hospital. The men returned home to North Adams, devastated by the tragic loss of the two young women.

John Widders was so distraught over the deaths of Mary and Sybil that he was placed on suicide watch. On the morning of August 2, Widders told the household staff that he was going out to the barn to check on the horses. A short while later he was found dead from a self-inflicted gunshot wound to the head. On August 11, ten days after the accident, Mr. Houghton passed away at home. The newspapers reported the cause of death as the result of injuries he received in the crash, but people who were close to the family say A. C. died of a broken heart.

In 1918 ownership of the mansion was passed to Florence (Houghton) Gallop and her husband, William. Two years later, the Gallops sold the property to the Masons and they built a Masonic Temple as an addition to the rear of the building. The Houghton Mansion is still used and maintained by the Lafayette Graylock Masonic Lodge A. F. & A. M. and the Naomi Chapter of the Eastern Star. For more than ninety years now, the Masons and their neighbors have believed that the mansion is indeed haunted by Mr. Houghton, his daughter Mary, and their faithful servant, John Widders.

Members of the Masonic Lodge started their own paranormal research group, Berkshire Paranormal, in 2004, when the ghostly activity in the building became too strange for them and their fellow brothers to ignore. The cofounders of the group are Josh Mantello and his father, Nick. The Mantellos have been with the Lodge for quite some time and have conducted countless hours of research in order to get the full story of the Houghtons and their former home. Josh is considered to be the "go-to-guy" for the mansion's ghost stories. He organizes the tours and paranormal events, which are open to the public throughout the year. On one of my visits to the mansion, I asked Josh to recall some of the most startling encounters he and others have had in the old building. Josh jokingly rolled his eyes and replied, "There are so many, I don't know where to begin."

The first thorough paranormal investigation of the Houghton Mansion was conducted by the Massachusetts-based New England Ghost Project at the request of Josh Mantello. Josh's own group was still in its infancy, so he thought it would be interesting to bring in an experienced team to see what they could find. The leader of N.E.G.P. is Ron Kolek, a well-liked and respected New England ghosthunter. I once accompanied Ron and his group on an investigation in the creepy Freetown

John Widders's room

State Forest and found them to be a sincere team who don't take themselves too seriously. After Josh Mantello informed me that N.E.G.P. was the first group to visit the mansion, I got in touch with Ron and asked him if anything strange had happened during their investigation. He told me he and his team had a few interesting moments that night, but there was one in particular that he will never forget. This is what Ron told me in his own words.

> It was late at night and we were up on the roof of the mansion. We were looking over North Adams, with all the spires, the churches, and the mountains. It was just me and another Mason by the name of Greg. We decided to go back in, so we started walking across the roof. Now, it had rained just a little while ago, so there were puddles. We got about halfway across the roof towards the stairs and all of a sudden we

*heard this sloshing, like footsteps in the water behind us, but
we were the only two up there. Just as we turned around, this
cold air came right by us. I had an EMF (electromagnetic
field) meter in my hand and it went off; it just totally spiked
as the cold rushed by us. It was a neat experience. We heard
something, felt something, and had a meter register something as well.*

The third floor of the mansion is where the servants' quarters were once located. There is a room at the back that is
believed to have been John Widders's quarters. This room has
only one window, which overlooks the back parking lot. When
Josh Mantello began putting together a Web site for the mansion, he took a series of pictures in and around the building to
upload to the new site. He found something startling in one of
the photographs when he transferred the pictures to his computer for better viewing. A shot taken at the back of the mansion
shows a white figure standing in the window of Widders' room.
What added to the mystery of this form standing at the window
was the state of the room at the time the picture was taken.
Widders's room was being used as a storage space for odds and
ends. As Josh explained, "There were two big glass domes for
light fixtures, pieces of plywood and junk just shoved into the
alcove in front of the window. I suppose someone could have
stood in front of the window if they had climbed over everything, but there were cobwebs running across, so you would
have been able to tell if someone had been standing there." The
photograph can be viewed at Berkshire Paranormal's Web site,
www.berkshireparanormal.com.

Widders's room has been a hot spot for paranormal activity.
Josh Mantello once watched a shadow figure move slowly across
the room while sitting on a vigil with two of his friends. His
fellow investigators were seated facing the other way, unaware

of what Josh was seeing. Josh said nothing to them. Instead, he slowly got up out of his chair and began to approach the dark form. Just as he did this, another friend, named Phil, entered the room. Phil and Josh both stopped in their tracks and looked at each other. After a short silence Phil asked Josh, "Did you see him too?"

They then asked Phil to leave the room and the three of them settled back down and waited. About ten minutes later, Josh and both his friends watched the double doors to the room's small closet open and close by itself. On a return visit in the summer of 2010, Ron Kolek and two female members of his group saw the same closet open by itself. One of the ladies then reported the sensation of being touched. A few minutes later, the door to the room opened with no one there. Ron and his team discounted the possibility of a breeze because they all had heard the handle turn as the door opened.

Mary Houghton's former room is located on the second floor. No one has ever reported seeing anything on this level of the mansion, but pictures taken in Mary's room have shown odd anomalies. People have been touched and sometimes pushed while seated in a certain chair. Others have felt an overwhelming sadness that has brought them to tears. The most impressive evidence captured in her room has been in the form of electronic voice phenomenon. Questions asked by investigators have often received direct responses such as "yes,' "no," and the ever popular "get out." Ghosthunter, Karen Mossey, captured a very clear EVP when she asked the spirit of A. C. Houghton if any of his children were in the house. The ghostly voice heard on her audio recorder answered back, "One is here."

The basement is another active area. It seems to be haunted by a young girl. No one has yet been able to connect this child to the Houghton family. There was a house on the property before the mansion was built, so it is safe to assume that the cellar hole to the original house was incorporated into the mansion's larger basement. Perhaps this little shade lived and died in the old house and is now haunting the only remnants of her family home. Her tiny footsteps have been heard as well as giggles and murmurs. The Mantellos and their fellow brothers have seen her dark shape moving around the basement many times. They have also seen small, colorful sparks of light flashing about them in the dark that they have nicknamed "sparklies."

In all the years that the Masons have held their meetings at the Houghton Mansion, nobody had ever experienced anything paranormal in the temple itself. However, Josh and other members of the lodge have conducted a few investigations in the temple and have had moments that left them wondering if former members are in fact visiting the temple from the other side. One instance involved a simple request for a sign that someone was there in the temple with them. Josh Mantello asked if someone could please help him finish tapping out "Shave and a haircut, two bits." Josh then knocked out the first five taps on the arm of the chair he was sitting in. He didn't receive two taps in response, but instead got two precise beeps from an electromagnetic field meter that had been placed on the other side of the room. With all the tragedy connected to the old mansion, it is nice to know that someone is still in good spirits.

Spotlight on: Charlemont Inn
Charlemont, Massachusetts

Charlemont, Massachusetts, is a very popular year-round destination for outdoor enthusiasts. Situated on the historic Mohawk Trail in the Berkshires, the area offers many great locations for hiking, camping, white water rafting, and skiing. A favorite spot in town to stay and to eat is the Charlemont Inn, which has been offering food and accommodations since 1787. Some of the notable figures who have stayed there include Mark Twain and President Calvin Coolidge.

It seems that a number of people who have either lodged at or worked in the inn during its long history are still there in spirit. Charlotte Dewey and Linda Shimandle are the co-owners of the inn. When Charlotte came into the business some twenty years ago, Linda, who had already been with the inn for some time, told her about the building's haunted reputation. Linda informed Charlotte that one of their ghosts is a mischievous teenager, whom she and the staff have affectionately nicknamed "Elizabeth."

Charlotte Dewey didn't put too much stock into the idea of ghosts until one morning when she walked into the kitchen and saw a bag of potato chips floating in midair. Stunned by this scene, Charlotte stopped dead in her tracks and said, "Elizabeth, put those down!" The bag of chips dropped to the floor on her command as Charlotte retreated with haste from the kitchen.

A prank the teenage ghost likes to play is the mysterious removal of personal items belonging to both guests and the staff. Two objects that disappear with frequency are eyeglasses and hairdryers. What use these articles have for a ghost on the other side of the spiritual veil is yet to be understood.

The Charlemont Inn has been visited by many mediums and psychics over the years, and some of them have hit upon the paranormal activity in the building with amazing accuracy. Charlotte

Spotlight on: Charlemont Inn
(continued)

Dewey told me that she likes to keep most of the ghost stories quiet, so as not to influence people. About five years ago, a woman with psychic ability visited the inn and informed the owners that there was a ghost of a fourteen-year-old girl who died of tuberculosis haunting the building. She didn't get the name Elizabeth. The name she got was Fidelia with the middle name Elvira.

The psychic also received the girl's last name. When a local woman volunteered to do research to see if there was any record of this girl, she found an exact match with the same age and cause of death. The woman was even able to locate the teenager's grave. Charlotte Dewey explained to me that she had to withhold the girl's last name from me out of respect for her descendants who still lived in the town of Charlemont. Further research showed that the Charlemont Inn was used during Fidelia's time as a place for local patients to meet with the regional physician. It is possible that Fidelia died at the inn while waiting for medical care.

More than a couple of psychics who have visited the inn have sensed the spirits of a little boy and girl, with a cat, hanging around near the bottom of the main staircase by the front desk. No one has ever seen these little wraiths, but members of the staff have commented on feeling a presence on the stairs, and some have even heard a cat in the same vicinity.

An apparition of a Colonial soldier has been seen on the second floor, but not of late. The room this ghost haunts is now used for storage and is seldom opened. A ghosthunting group took photographs inside the storeroom and captured strange distortions that they believed to be evidence of a vortex or doorway into the spirit world. One of the guestrooms on the second floor is also notorious for providing photographic anomalies. A guest once took a picture of this room and noticed there was an image of a tic-tac-toe game within the mirror. When the mirror was examined, no explanation could be found for it. Nothing was discovered on or behind the glass to account for the phantom marks.

A guest who stays regularly at the inn during hunting season had an experience in that same room that caused him to leave for the woods much earlier then usual. It was around four o'clock in the morning when Charlotte Dewey saw this man come down the stairs and head for the front door. She could see that he was badly shaken and immediately asked him why he was up and leaving so early. The man was ashen and couldn't form a coherent sentence but said he would explain later. When the guest was finally able to talk to Charlotte about his rapid departure, he told her that he had been woken up by being pelted with little bars of guest soap. When he jumped up out of his bed, he could see no one responsible for the toiletry attack. The man then noticed there was a full-body impression on the mattress of the unused bed in the room. This was too much, especially since he had checked into the room alone. The hunter decided it would be a lot safer in the woods, so he headed for the hills as fast as his legs could take him.

CHAPTER 8

Ventfort Hall Mansion and Gilded Age Museum
LENOX, MASSACHUSETTS

DURING THE PERIOD between the American Civil War and World War I, known as the Gilded Age, Lenox, Massachusetts, was a popular seasonal retreat for many talented celebrities and wealthy industrialists. The sheer beauty of the area inspired the rich and famous to buy land there and build grand summer homes for their vacations in the social season. In 1891 Sarah Morgan (sister of the powerful financier J. P. Morgan) and her husband, George, bought twenty-six acres and hired the famous Boston architects Rotch and Tilden to design and build a fifty-room mansion in the Jacobean Revival style at a cost of $900,000.

The Morgans' summer retreat was felt by many to be one the loveliest homes in town. The red-brick-and-brownstone building contained the very latest in modern conveniences available at the time. Features included gas and electric lights, central heating, burglar alarms, and an elevator. Along with the fifteen bedrooms, thirteen bathrooms, and seventeen fireplaces, the hall also had a two-lane bowling alley located in the basement. This luxurious home was once surrounded by beautifully landscaped gardens. George Morgan was a horticulturalist and he maintained six greenhouses on the property. Sadly, his gardens are gone now. Over time the grounds have been reduced to less than twelve acres and only the back lawn remains.

After the Morgans passed away, the house was rented to Mrs. Margaret Vanderbilt, a widow who had lost her husband in 1915 when the ocean liner RMS *Lusitania* sank, torpedoed by a German U-boat. From 1925 to 1945, W. Roscoe Bonsal owned the property. He was involved with the expansion of the railways in the southeast. After the Bonsals left Ventfort Hall, the building had many owners. In the 1980s the house fell into the hands of a developer who intended to raze the place to make way for a nursing home. Those plans fell through, but that didn't stop the developer from stripping the building of its valuable fixtures, including the entire bowling alley.

The hall began to rapidly deteriorate. A section of the roof collapsed, allowing the elements and animals to damage the building even further. In 1994 the Ventfort Hall Association (VHA) was formed with the goal of saving this splendid piece of history. Three years later, the association obtained the property through private donations and a loan from the National Trust for Historic Preservation. The VHA has quite a task on its hands, but through hard work and perseverance the VHA is making great progress. Ventfort Hall is now beginning to reflect the charm and character it once held in the Morgans' time.

In the ten years since the Ventfort Hall Mansion and Gilded Age Museum opened to the public, staff members have had a number of occasions that made them stop and wonder about paranormal activity at the mansion. Doors opening and closing, the sound of footsteps, disembodied voices and shadowy figures have been perceived at times when everyone in the building was accounted for. A former office manager was seated at her desk one morning when she became enveloped by the pleasant scent of lilac perfume. There were no flowers inside or outside the office. The windows were not open and the cleaning lady assured the manager that she had not been using any kind of flower-scented cleaners. The smell of flowers is often reported in haunted locations. What makes it so strange is that the scent will come on strong, suddenly, and then it will disappear without a trace.

Some members of the VHA have reported the sensation of being touched: not shoved, but gently stroked. One afternoon, a male staff member (he requested his name not be used) was helping with an event at the museum in which a classical pianist was performing for guests in the great hall. As he stood to the back of the large audience, overseeing the affair, he felt a hand touch his back. He said it was as if a loved one had stepped up next to him and placed a hand on his back to show affection. When he turned to see who was touching him, no one was there.

I became aware of Ventfort Hall and its haunted reputation when Tom Laughlin of Chicopee Paranormal Investigators (CPI) contacted me. Tom had found my Web site and wanted to know if I would be interested in joining his team on an investigation at the museum. The Ventfort Hall Association had asked CPI to conduct investigations at the hall to collect any evidence that might support the claims of their staff and board members. Tom and his group jumped at the opportunity, and I happily accepted Tom's invitation.

The Library Room, where clear recordings of electronic voice phenomenon (EVP) have been recorded by Chicopee Paranormal Investigators.

I arrived at Ventfort Hall on a cloudless, moonlit night in November 2010. Tom Laughlin greeted me at the mansion's striking coach-gate entrance; the setting was perfect for a paranormal investigation. Tom then introduced me to the members of his team, Tania Mega; Matt Deprey; and a friend of theirs named Chris, who had tagged along for the adventure; and Mark Monette, the group tour coordinator at the hall since 2009. Mark was there that night not only to let us into the museum, but also to join in on the investigation. Mark had taken part in all the previous ghosthunts conducted by CPI and was especially curious about what Tom's group might find because he, too, has had some strange experiences in the old building.

While the team got their equipment ready for the night, I asked Mark to tell me about the strange things he has witnessed at the hall. He began with a winter night in 2009: "The building was empty; we had already closed down for the day, and the former office manager and I were the only two in the building. I had closed up the second floor and closed all the doors; it is part of the routine at night. We were getting ready to leave and we had shut off the lights in the office. We were walking out into the hallway and all of a sudden we heard the sound of someone upstairs in boots or maybe high heels going, *clomp, clomp, clomp* and then *slam!* We both turned and looked at each other and I said, 'Is there anyone in the house that you know of?' and the office manager said, 'No.' so then I had to go up there and check. I was a little sketched out as I looked around, but found no one up there, and all the doors were still closed. I couldn't find any explanation for the sounds. We pretty much flew out of here!"

The second odd moment for Mark happened only a week before my visit. He was in the library on a Saturday morning, cleaning up from the previous night's activities. He was moving a table when he heard a soft thud, accompanied by a faint clink of glass. When he turned around, he immediately noticed a candle in the middle of the floor. The candle was from the center of a candelabra that Mark had moved to the safety of a shelf only a few moments before. The sound of glass came from the bobeche (a ring placed around the bottom of a candle to catch the melting wax), which was still in place around the base of the candle. The candle was more than ten feet from the wall where Mark had placed it, and neither the candle nor the delicate piece of crystal showed any signs of damage.

Tom Laughlin shared with me some video and audio clips that were recorded by his group on their previous visits to Ventfort Hall. Unfortunately, CPI's video cameras have not yet captured the image of a ghost at the hall, but the microphones on their cameras and handheld recorders have caught some fascinating examples of electronic voice phenomenon (EVP).

One night, while sitting in a room on the second floor, the

group members heard the sound of someone walking softly in the hallway. Nobody was found to be there. Later, when they reviewed the audio recording that was made at the moment the footsteps were heard, they discovered a child-like voice calling out, "Hello?" Another remarkable EVP was heard on a recorder that was left running in the hallway on the first floor. The team had gathered downstairs for a coffee break and when they finished, everyone moved up to the second floor to resume the evening's investigation. Not long after the first floor had grown quiet, a voice was recorded in the hallway saying, "Need some more coffee."

Another of the video clips was shot in the library by a camera that was left running in the room. Shortly after Tom Laughlin left the library and shut the doors, the video camera's microphone captured a voice saying, "He's gone." Then a second voice asks, "Where's Sally?" Then, what sounds like the first voice answering back, "I don't know." Research has uncovered the fact that George Morgan's second wife, who was also named Sarah, was nicknamed Sally.

Perhaps the most intriguing moment for CPI occurred on their first investigation of the museum. The group was sitting around in the basement room that once housed the bowling alley. As Tom Laughlin and the others took turns trying to lure out a ghost, the door to the old bowling alley opened slightly. Everyone then tried to encourage whoever was there to come inside, but the door instead closed. When Tom opened the door, they saw a strange light disappear quickly into the maze of rooms that make up the basement area. Those who briefly saw the light agreed it was nothing like a flashlight. Stranger still, the video camera failed to pick out the light and caught only Tom's shocked reaction. A skeptical VHA board member tried to find a rational explanation for the door opening, but failed to do so and dropped the subject.

The night I was there, Tom, Matt Deprey, and I ventured down into the basement and staked out the old bowling alley. We shut the door and set up a device referred to as a laser star light. It has the appearance of a standard flashlight, but instead of a single, white beam, it emits several dozen pinpoints of purple light. These pinpoints create what looks like a star field in the darkened room. The idea behind this gadget is that if anything should pass through its beams, the movement will stand out to the naked eye.

While we stood there quietly using our own five senses to detect any change in the room, Matt Deprey's electromagnetic field detector gave off a short reaction. Matt is an electrician by trade and could find no explanation as to why his meter had just registered a short flux. A few moments later, I thought I saw a dark shadow move through the beams. I said nothing. Another moment later, I saw it again, but this time Matt saw it too and spoke up. The three of us then stood still, waiting to see if there would be any more movement. I turned to look at Tom and as I did, he let out a little shriek and wiped his face with his free hand. Tom said, "Turn on a light! Is there something hanging from the ceiling?" Our flashlight showed nothing, not even a cobweb. Tom said he had felt a soft stroke on his left check. As we settled down from his amusing outburst, the door to the room opened half way.

I realize that what I saw in the basement is not proof that Ventfort Hall is haunted, but just like the skeptical board member who could find no clear explanation for what happened during CPI's first investigation, I will leave it alone and let others decide for themselves.

Rhode Island

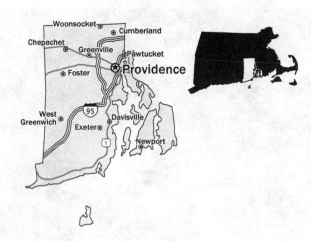

Chepachet
Tavern on Main
The Village of Chepachet

Cumberland
Nine Men's Misery

Davisville
Quonset Air Museum

Exeter
Chestnut Hill Cemetery

Foster
Hopkins Mills
Moosup Valley

Greenville
Stillwater Antiques

Newport
Belcourt Castle

Pawtucket
Slater Mill Museum

West Greenwich
Historic Cemetery Number Two

Woonsocket
St. Ann Arts and Cultural Center

CHAPTER 9

Quonset Air Museum
DAVISVILLE, RHODE ISLAND

Grumman F–14 Tomcat with its distinctive "Grim Reaper" tail marking

HAVE YOU EVER HEARD OF A QOUNSET HUT? If not, you more than likely have seen one in a photograph or documentary about World War II. They're those round, prefab buildings with a tall, arched roof made from corrugated steel. The Quonset hut was found in every theater of the war, and its simplistic design can still be seen in use today all over the world. It was created in Davisville, Rhode Island, at the Quonset Point Naval Air Station in response to the Allies' need for a strong, simple design structure that could be easily transported and assembled anywhere the military had to be. The task of building bases with these fine examples of Yankee ingenuity fell into the hands of the "Fighting Seabees." Those brave combat engineers have their roots firmly planted in Quonset Point as well. Their iconic logo—a Tommy-gun-toting bumble bee wearing a sailor's cap and holding a tool in each of his six hands—was also created there by a civilian designer, named Frank Lafrate.

I once received an email about a haunted Quonset hut located in the quiet hamlet of Moosup Valley, Rhode Island. A woman named Beth told me she lived in the hut for a short time and had heard the unmistakable sound of someone wearing boots walk from one end of her apartment to the other. She heard this on many occasions. A relative moved into the hut right after Beth and reported hearing the same sound herself. The one question I put to Beth was, "Did the hut come from the old base at Davisville?" The answer was yes; her grandfather had bought it as a temporary living space for the family while he built their new home. I had my answer as to why the place was haunted.

What I mean by that is, I have an understanding of just how much death and loss there has been at the former naval base. In my late teens, I built in-ground swimming pools with an older guy named Angelo, who would tell me stories about when he worked at the base during the Second World War. Injuries to one of his hands and an ankle as a young boy kept him out of military service, so he got a job at Quonset Point sorting out all the damaged, battle-scarred vehicles and equipment coming back from the Mediterranean and European theaters. Angelo would describe to me how much bloody evidence of death there was to be found while inspecting the shot-up jeeps, trucks, and aircraft for evaluation and repairs. I'll never forget the look on his face as he recalled the many times he saw piles of sheepskin flight suits, all full of bullet holes, shrapnel tears, and blood. I sometimes wonder if a few spirits of the brave men who died fighting in, on, or around that war-battered equipment might have somehow bonded with it out of some strong sense of duty and responsibility and simply followed their vehicles, weapons, and machines back to the naval airbase.

Quonset Point has seen military activity since as far back as the War for Independence. Men were positioned here along the shoreline to watch out for British raiders in Narragansett Bay. By the late nineteenth century, Quonset Point had become the state's campground for military drill and training. In May of 1940, Rear Admiral Hepburn selected the location as the ideal place for a naval airbase, so neighboring land was taken by the government to expand the installation. Two Colonial-era cemeteries had to be moved to make way for the new construction. The human remains were exhumed as well as they could be and then transported to nearby Quidnessett Cemetery for reburial. What was recovered of those long-decomposed bodies was deposited into a mass grave, then adorned with a large stone marker to explain the necessity for the change in burial location.

I have heard more than a few stories about people seeing strange lights and shadows moving around the memorial and the sad grave it marks. It is possible that some of the people who were moved from their original family plot are not at rest. They could be unhappy with the new location and the conditions of their mass grave. There is also the gruesome fact that not all of their remains made it to the second burial site. A measure of their essence is still in the ground, somewhere, back at the old base.

From World War II to the Korean War and all the way through the Viet Nam War, the Quonset Point Naval Air Station served the United States proudly as an outstanding training facility for military aviators. If it has flown in the service of the United States military, it has flown in and out of Quonset Point. Despite the Navy's long history with Davisville, it saw fit to deactivate the Quonset Point Naval Air Station in 1974. Mostly an industrial business park today, it is still home to the Quonset Point Air National

A three-quarter scale replica of an F6F Hellcat. The man who built this airplane passed away before he had a chance to see it fly. Perhaps his anxious spirit is responsible for the footsteps that are heard pacing around inside the hanger at night.

Guard Station and the R.I. Army National Guard stations their Blackhawk helicopters there. Every June, the base is host to the Quonset Air Show, a very big event that draws thousands of aviation enthusiasts from all over southern New England.

In 1992, through efforts made by former Rhode Island Governor Bruce Sundlun, the Quonset Air Museum got underway as a serious endeavor to not only restore and display rare examples of important aircraft, but to also preserve the proud history of the former naval air station for generations to come. Governor Sundlun served as the captain of a B-17 Flying Fortress in the war over Europe and was shot down. Being a Jewish-American bomber pilot on the run in Nazi-held territory could not have been fun. But he made it; he beat the odds.

Another Rhode Islander who beat the odds in aerial combat is George Sutcliffe. George is a fighter ace who flew the P-47

Thunderbolt. I see him in my local supermarket from time to time. One afternoon, he caught sight of me in a T-shirt I bought as a souvenir of the time I took a flight in a B-24 Liberator. George came up to me, pointed at my shirt, and told me his brother was the copilot on one, and his captain was none other than Jimmy Stewart, the movie star. Every day this country loses more and more of these exceptional men from a generation like no other. As some of them depart this world, are they leaving something of themselves behind? The Quonset Air Museum may be the place to find an answer to that question.

I ponder this thought with David Payne, the air museum's president, in a small room that has been made to resemble an Air Force ready room. The Spartan room is used for special functions, like birthday parties and meetings. The walls are decorated with paintings by local artist Domenic Denardo. The images in oil paint depict some of the most amazing documented moments in military aviation. Actions involving Bruce Sundlun and George Sutcliffe are the subjects for two of Denardo's works. David Payne told me the room is dedicated to the memory of a gentleman who used to spend a lot of time at the museum. His name was Lt. Colonel William Hunter. He flew a B-17 in the 97th Bomb Group under the command of Paul Tibbets and received the Silver Star for action taken in the air over enemy territory. Lt. Colonel Hunter loved to hang out at the museum and talk shop. His favorite aircraft on display was the Navy C-1A because it is powered by the same engines as Hunter's old B-17. David says he and others get a positive vibe whenever they are in this little room. He can sometimes feel William Hunter's presence and for him "that's a good thing."

The air museum sits on three acres of land with its main building taking up 200 by 180 feet of that space. The building was built in 1945 as a place to wash and paint aircraft. There were six huge heaters mounted to the walls that used fans to dry the planes after being washed and then again after they were painted. There are tunnels beneath the base that also run under the museum. As David pointed out to me, they could be the explanation for some of the voices he and the volunteers have heard at night when the place is still. But not all of them. He has had more than a few moments in the old building that have left him wondering about who could still be there and why. While walking around the static displays, David mentions the fact that all of the museum's helicopters saw service in Viet Nam. The horrors the crews of those aircraft saw one can only imagine. He also brought up the number of known deaths in the base's history—six hundred men lost in training exercises. Any one of them could still be around, carrying out his daily routines and duties, unaware of his sudden and violent death.The locations where David has had the most experiences are in the back of the building, in the machine shops and storage areas. David some-times uses one of the backrooms when he works on the muse-um's archives. He has been back there in the evening and heard voices he can't place and the unmistakable sound of shoes scuff-ing the concrete floor. He has heard these sounds so often that his reaction to them now is to just say, "Hi, how's it going?"

David and the staff have yet to see the most tantalizing piece of evidence of the museum's haunting. A visitor took a picture of one of the planes displayed outside. The man who took the picture tried to tell David all about it, but because he was so busy with everything going on that day, he didn't have a chance to get the story clear or set up a time for the man to bring the photograph in for closer examination. The photographer claims that there is someone sitting in the cockpit of one of the planes. At the time the picture was taken, the museum did not have any mannequins seated in any of the aircraft. If it is the plane Dave thinks it is, the canopy is screwed shut; no one could have gotten into it.

Parts to a World War II F6F Hellcat fighter that is undergoing restoration. Some members of the air museum wonder if this wreckage is haunted by the plane's last pilot.

One of the few planes on display that is able to fly has never flown. It is a three-quarter-scale replica of an F6 Hellcat. The man who built it passed away a few years ago and never saw it fly, which is something he very much wanted to see. "If Al is around, he's pissed because we haven't got it to fly yet. My goal is to get the wheels off the ground and then put it back in here and hang it up." David says. Behind the replica are pieces of an actual Hellcat that crashed in 1944. Dave wonders if the late pilot, Vincent A. Frankwitz, is still attached to the wreckage.

There are a few other candidates for spiritual visitation at the museum. A couple of local vets who volunteered their time and knowledge to the museum have passed away in recent years. David says it straight from the shoulder. "These guys are here. I don't care what you think. You go by these planes and you feel something."

Spotlight On:
Chestnut Hill Cemetery
Exeter, Rhode Island

The Chestnut Hill Baptist Church stands upon a rise alongside Route 102 in the town of Exeter, Rhode Island. Built in 1838, the building is a simple wooden structure that was constructed in the Greek Revival style. It is a handsome example of an old New England church, but what the church is best known for is its cemetery and the grave of America's last vampire.

Throughout the eighteenth and nineteenth centuries, New England was in the grasp of the terrible disease tuberculosis, referred to then as consumption. The illness takes its victims slowly; they waste away as if their life force was being sucked out of them. These symptoms were interpreted by European settlers as the work of a vaporous vampire that would repeatedly invade a person's body during the night until all their life essence was gone. They also believed that the vampire would later conceal itself in that person's dead body and use their grave as a hiding place from which to strike, continuing its evil work on another member of the family or community.

The last recorded case of this superstitious hysteria involved the Brown family of Exeter, Rhode Island, in 1892. George Brown lost his wife, Mary, to consumption and one of his daughters, Olive. When his only son, Edwin, became ill he was encouraged to travel to Colorado for treatment. While Edwin was away, his sister, Mercy, was struck by the disease and died before he could return home. Some residents of the town began to pressure George Brown to look into the possibility of a vampire lurking in their midst that was responsible for the deaths of his wife and two daughters.

George Brown didn't believe in the vampire theory and was horrified by his neighbors' recommendation that he dig up his wife and daughter to see if either of their bodies were being used

Spotlight On:
Chestnut Hill Cemetery
(continued)

as vessels to harbor a vampire. Mercy Brown had died during the winter so her body was still in the cemetery's crypt awaiting burial when the ground thawed in the spring. Brown wanted no part of his neighbor's wild suggestions. Doctor Harold Metcalf of Wickford, Rhode Island, felt the same as Mr. Brown, but several people in the town of Exeter were upset that nothing was being done to end the curse of a vampire they truly believed was going to kill them all. Something had to be done to end their fears.

In March of 1892, with George Brown absent, Doctor Metcalf went to the Chestnut Hill Cemetery with a small group of locals to settle the matter once and for all. Mary and Olive Brown's graves were dug up, and the remains of both of them were in an advanced state of decay. The grim party then moved to the crypt to examine Mercy. Because her body was found in seemingly fresh condition, the fearful members of the group believed they had unmasked their vampire.

The doctor tried to explain that Mercy's body showed all the normal signs of decay to be expected with a body that had been stored through the winter, but the vampire hunters didn't want to hear his explanations. They demanded that her heart be cut out, burned, and the ashes fed to Edwin Brown as a cure for his sickness. Doctor Metcalf went along with their wishes, but it changed nothing. Edwin Brown eventually died from consumption and was buried in the family plot.

Besides this bizarre chapter in Rhode Island history, there have been many reports over the years of people seeing strange, blue lights in the church graveyard. My colleague Pamela Patalano showed me some photographs that were given to her by her friend

Gary. He claims that he and his friends had stopped at the Chestnut Hill Cemetery in October 2009 on the spur of the moment because it was close to Halloween, and they had heard a vampire was buried there. That is all they knew of the legend, nothing else.

As they approached the center of the cemetery, Gary and his friends noticed what looked like little blue lights glowing on the ground before some of the gravestones. As they walked closer, the lights faded and disappeared. In a few moments the lights reappeared, but now they were at the back of the cemetery and floating about in the night air. The pictures Gary had taken showed what looked like common dust or moisture orbs caught by the camera's flash. Pam and Gary agree, but Gary assured us that the smaller points of blue light caught by his camera were what he and his friends saw that night with their own eyes. I found Gary's story and pictures to be very interesting, considering the fact that he and his friends had never heard anything about the reports of phantom blue lights in the Chestnut Hill Cemetery.

CHAPTER 10

Slater Mill Museum

PAWTUCKET, RHODE ISLAND

TWENTY-ONE-YEAR-OLD SAMUEL SLATER came to America in 1789, determined to build and operate his own cotton-spinning mill. He had gained seven years of experience in the business through an apprenticeship with a mill owner named Jedediah Strutt back in Belpur, England. Strutt's mill was designed by Richard Arkwright, a pioneer in the processing of raw cotton into fine thread through the use of water-powered machinery. Slater understood that his own hands-on knowledge of Arkwright's cutting-edge technology and design would give him a great advantage over anyone working with textiles in America.

In 1790 he moved to Pawtucket, Rhode Island, and started a partnership with Moses Brown, the abolitionist from Providence. Three years later, with financial backing from Brown and his partners, Samuel Slater built what would become the first successful, water-powered cotton-spinning mill in America. Slater's factory system was quickly embraced by many in the local textile business. Over the next thirty years, nearly one hundred water-powered mills were built along the banks of the Blackstone River from Worcester, Massachusetts, to Providence, Rhode Island. This period of rapid, industrial growth in the Blackstone Valley would mark the beginning of the American Industrial Revolution.

Samuel Slater would become one of the richest men in the United States. In a speech paying tribute to the industrialist, President Andrew Jackson gave Slater the moniker "Father of American Manufactures." Slater's factory style, also referred to as "The Rhode Island Style," brought the concept of the English mill town to America. Families were encouraged to work and live as a community alongside the business. Employees were paid with company script, a form of currency that could only be used to purchase goods at the company's store. It was a hard and bleak existence for those who lived the life of a mill worker, especially for the children. Boys and girls as young as seven years of age worked in the mills. Because of their small size, the children were given the dangerous job of climbing in and around the looms to load new spools or to set jammed parts free. Many horrible accidents happened in the textile industry of this period, and Slater Mill was no exception. Unfortunately, severed fingers and torn limbs were common occurrences for those working around the water-powered machinery. When one considers all the blood, sweat, and tears that have been shed over Slater Mill's long history, it seems the perfect place to be haunted.

When all business at the mill ceased in 1921, a group of local businesspeople formed the Old Slater Mill Association and bought the property. In 1925, they reopened Slater Mill as a museum about the American textile industry, in the very place where it all began. The Slater Mill building was declared a National Historic Landmark in 1966, but when the other two buildings on the property (the Wilkinson Mill and the Sylvanus Brown House) were restored and opened in the early 1970s, the status was changed to National Historic Landmark District. Over the many decades since the museum first opened, no one had ever documented any stories about the place being haunted. That changed one evening in 2005 when staff members had to deal with people they couldn't see.

It was closing time and the museum's educational director was setting the motion-sensor alarms in the Slater Mill building, which was something he had done many times. On this particular night, he was having difficulty arming the system. He checked to see if there were any doors or windows left open and also made sure that there was no one left behind in the building. Nothing was found to be out of place. The director tried to set the system again, but was still unable to arm the alarm for the night. When he contacted the company that monitors the museum's alarm system, he was told: "The sensors indicate you have a group of people walking around on the second floor." When the director went upstairs he could find no explanation for what the sensors were detecting. The alarm company was certain that their sensors were picking up the movement of people and not an animal, like a rat or a stray cat. The alarm company sent their technicians to check the motion sensors the following day, and they could find no fault in the system.

About a month after this happened, a good friend and colleague of mine, Carl Johnson, began working at Slater Mill as an interpreter. He learned of the educational director's dealings

The Sylvanus Brown House. The ghost of a young girl, called Becca, haunts this old home.

with the phantoms on the second floor after he too detected people moving around up there one night after closing. Carl was sweeping the first floor in the Slater Mill building when he became aware of people moving about and talking softly on the floor above him. He continued on with his work, all the time wondering who was still in the building at that hour. When Carl went upstairs to look for the people that he clearly heard only moments ago, he found no one. There was no way anyone could have come down from the second floor and left the building without him seeing or hearing them do so.

Carl's twin brother, Keith, also works at Slater Mill as an interpretive guide. The Johnson brothers are not only local history buffs, they are also well-known and respected ghosthunters here in southern New England. They have been investigating the paranormal for more than thirty years. Not long after Carl had his experience, the twins began investigating the historic mill site for solid evidence of ghosts. They have since come to believe that Slater Mill is indeed haunted.

The Johnsons conduct public ghost tours at Slater Mill in the autumn. These nighttime sojourns give moderately sized groups the opportunity to tour all three buildings and hear the many tales of strange happenings reported by museum staff and visitors. Guests of these tours are encouraged to bring their own cameras and audio recorders to try to catch spirit activity. To some, this may sound like a pedestrian way to conduct a paranormal investigation, but beginner's luck has paid out on these tours. A few of these first-time investigators have found anomalies in their photographs and unexplainable voices on their recorders. Several people have also seen apparitions.

A male figure has been seen in the Slater Mill building more than once. On the night of May 28, 2009, members of the tour saw his dark form near the gift shop. While standing outside the building on Halloween night, 2008, Carl noticed that the lights on the second floor were turned back on. He was absolutely certain he had turned off all the lights before moving his group on to the next part of the tour. He and eight other witnesses saw a man walking about in the now-lighted room. Carl went back into the locked building to find out who the man was and how he got in, but there was nobody to be found.

The museum's paranormal activity isn't exclusive to the ghost tours; there have been some very spooky moments that have taken place during the day. In April 2007 Carl was conducting a tour of the mill's first floor when he was interrupted by what sounded like a boy screaming. Everyone was accounted for and no injured child could be found either inside or outside of the building. Carl told me, "If I had to pinpoint a location, it came from the bell tower."

The Sylvanus Brown House, built in 1758, was brought to the mill site in 1962 to save it from demolition. Samuel Slater spent his first four nights in Pawtucket as a guest in this house, so it made a perfect addition to the museum grounds. It appears to be haunted by a little girl dressed in white. On September 19, 2008, a woman walked around to the back of the small house to view the spice and herb garden. The visitor was facing the back of the house when she noticed a young girl in one of the gambrel windows, looking down at her. The woman turned her attention back to the garden, but feeling a little uneasy looked back to the window. The girl was still there. Shortly after walking away form the back of the house, the visitor saw Carl Johnson and told him about the girl she had just seen. Even though Johnson knew the house was locked and no one could have been in there, he asked the woman if she thought the girl could have been one of the other guides dressed in period costume. She assured him that the girl was definitely a child. "I know the lady was sincere," said Carl, "because her bottom lip was trembling." This wraith was seen again during the daytime by a young man who was taking a tour inside the house. While the guide was speaking to the group about the home's history, the young man watched this peculiar little girl in white walk soundlessly from the bedroom to the adjoining loom room. No one else on the tour took any notice of her, so he said nothing about it until a short time later when he asked, "Is this place haunted?"

The voice of a young girl has been heard in the house quite a few times. On two different nights, paranormal investigators asked the girl for her name. Both teams caught the same EVP (electronic voice phenomenon) of a young girl giving the name, Becca, which is most likely short for Rebecca. This name has not been found in any research conducted on the home's history. She could possibly be one of the orphaned children who worked at the mill and perhaps lost her life in an accident that was never recorded. The deaths of children in textile mills were never recorded; it was considered bad for the industry's image.

The third building on the site is the massive Wilkinson Mill. Slater's partner built this rubble-stone-and-granite structure to act as the service station for the business. Its machine shop was powered by a sixteen-thousand-pound water wheel, which is still in operation today. Visitors and staff standing outside the building have observed a man in dark gray work clothes walking past the windows. There are no interpreters at the mill who wear such attire. This figure, like the others, makes itself scarce when anyone tries to find him.

One evening in November 2009, Carl Johnson was taking a small group of ghosthunters through the machine shop. He began calling out to whomever might be present in spirit form to show themselves so that they might be photographed. As he was speaking, one member of the tour shot several pictures in the dimly lighted room. What the man caught with his camera can only be described by Carl as something "smoky and feathery" forming in the air. Guests of the ghost tours can examine copies of these pictures.

One night in May 2009, some young ladies who were taking a break on a bench outside of the Wilkinson Mill saw the man in gray. They watched this translucent, gray man move quickly up the stairs to the workshop and disappear as he reached the door. The rest of the girls' friends were with Carl inside the shop. These two groups were startled to learn that they had both seen this figure at the same time—only Carl's group saw him enter the shop without making any sound and simply blink out of sight. Apparently, not even death can keep these souls from their work at Slater Mill.

Spotlight On: Nine Men's Misery Cumberland, Rhode Island

On March 26, 1676, ten Colonial militiamen were captured by a group of Narragansett Indians after a horrible battle that took place during King Philip's War. The Indians had lured Captain Michael Pierce and eighty of his soldiers (twenty of whom were Christian Indians) to an area that is known today as Central Falls, Rhode Island. Captain Pierce believed that he was pursuing a small force of exhausted natives who could be easily dealt with. He was wrong. It was a clever trap that led to the deaths of Pierce and nearly all of his men.

The ten militiamen were caught as they tried to retreat from the fight and were taken to a place referred to as "Camp Swamp." One of the men escaped captivity, but the other nine men were skinned alive and chopped into pieces by the Narragansetts who were hell-bent on revenge for the atrocities committed by the English during the "Great Swamp Fight" in Kingston, Rhode Island. When English

The Nine Men's Misery Memorial

Spotlight On: Nine Men's Misery
(continued)

reinforcements finally arrived they found the mutilated remains of the nine men and placed them in a mass grave and placed a stone cairn atop it as a grave marker. Since then the spot has been called, "The Nine Men's Misery."

In the early 1900s the property was purchased by an order of Trappist monks, who built a monastery within walking distance of the mass grave. They constructed a simple stone monument (in the shape of a loaf of bread) at the site, and in 1928 the Rhode Island Historical Society placed a marker in front of the monument. This is supposedly the oldest memorial to fallen soldiers in North America. The Cistercian Monastery burned down in 1950, and the land now belongs to the town of Cumberland. Public walking trails lead to the monument.

Many people believe that the woods and swamp around the Nine Men's Misery is haunted. People have reported hearing the screams of the tortured men coming from the gravesite. In the 1960s a volunteer with the Rhode Island Historical Society found boxes stored in the basement of the society's headquarters containing some bones and nine human skulls. The remains were labeled as being from the Nine Men's Misery and had apparently been removed during an archeological dig at the site in the early twentieth century. The bones were reinterred at the monument soon after the shocking discovery by the volunteer. This desecration may have upset the souls of the nine militiamen, causing their unrest.

The ghost of a little girl has also been seen in the vicinity of the Nine Men's Misery. On one of my visits to the area I noticed that a mill once stood about one hundred yards from the mass grave. I was told that the mill was built and operated by David Wilkinson, the man who later became partners with Samuel Slater, the father of the American Industrial Revolution. It was common for mills to be staffed with young children, and it is a sad fact that many of them were injured or killed while working on and around the dangerous water-powered machinery. Perhaps this ghostly child is a forgotten victim from the days when the mill was in operation.

Another haunting reported in the woods is the sound of horses galloping about and whinnying. Harle Tinney from Belcourt Castle in Newport, Rhode Island, told me that her in-laws used to own the farmland near the Nine Men's Misery and the site of the old mill. She said her late mother-in-law, Ruth Tinney, would rescue unwanted horses and bring them to the family's farm for a better life. When the horses passed away, they were buried in a special place on the farm. It could be that Ruth Tinney's horses are still running free on the old farm where they were loved and cared for.

It should also be mentioned that the Cumberland Public Library, which was incorporated into the remains of the old monastery, is haunted too. The activity is reported to occur in the older section of the building, and there are claims of a ghostly monk walking the grounds around the library.

CHAPTER 11

St. Ann Arts and Cultural Center
WOONSOCKET, RHODE ISLAND

SHORTLY AFTER THE START of the American Industrial Revolution in Pawtucket, Rhode Island, water-powered mills and factories began appearing all along the banks of the Blackstone River, turning the whole region into a hub for the textile industry. In northern Rhode Island, the agricultural community of Woonsocket Falls was transformed from a small village into the city of Woonsocket in only a few decades. Except for a lull during the Great Depression, Woonsocket prospered from the textile business until the end of World War II. Since then, the city has moved with the times and become home to a number of manufacturers and companies developing new technologies. Woonsocket is a classic example of an old New England mill town, with French-Canadians playing an important role in the city's history. The first of their numbers to arrive in the area had left their farms in Quebec during the mid-nineteenth century to look for work in the factories along the Blackstone River. These hardworking immigrants were also devout Christians who felt a strong desire to have a proper place of worship in their growing, close-knit community.

In 1913 this determined group of working-class citizens began construction of Saint Ann's Roman Catholic Church. They had no wealthy sponsors to fund this monumental endeavor, so all the money required for the project was raised by the parishioners themselves. The construction of the building was completed by 1917: The result is a splendid church in the modern French Renaissance Style. During the 1920s more than forty stained-glass windows were designed, crafted, and installed by artists in Chartres, France. Marble imported from Carrara, Italy, formed the church's altar.

The most impressive features of Saint Ann's are the frescos covering the interior walls, vaults, and ceilings. They were painted by the famed Italian artist Guidi Nincheri and are the largest collection of frescos in North America. Nincheri used the same sixteenth-century technique as Michelangelo, and in keeping with the Renaissance tradition, he depicted members of the community in his work.

By the later half of the twentieth century, the number of parishioners at Saint Ann's started to decline. In the year 2000, the Diocese of Providence decided to close the church due to the rising cost of its maintenance. Concerned that this sad step might lead to demolition, a dedicated group of people came together to save this beautiful, historic landmark. They formed the St. Ann Arts and Cultural Center and began leasing the building. In 2007 the Diocese of Providence gave ownership of the building to this nonprofit organization, which now offers the building to the public as a venue for local art and cultural activities. Not long after Saint Ann's took on its new role as an arts and cultural center, the board members and their volunteers became aware that they were not the only ones on the premises who care deeply for this remarkable church.

I first heard about the cultural center's haunted reputation from a paranormal investigator named Charles Reis, who is the vice-president of the University of Rhode Island Ghost Hunting Team. Reis has conducted two investigations of the building with U.R.I.G.H.T. and believes it is haunted. He showed me a photograph that he took with a digital camera in the basement of the church that appears to show a shadowy figure. Charles tried to duplicate the photograph to see if there was an explanation for the shadow, but he could not recreate the dark form.

With my interest piqued, I asked Charles if I could meet with him at Saint Ann's to talk with some of the board members who have also experienced unexplainable events in the building. Charles arranged the meeting and invited his colleagues, John Hardy and Fran Ford, to join us as well. John and Fran took part in U.R.G.H.T.'s investigations at the old church and recorded what they believe are electronic voice phenomenon (EVP), or spirit voices. Not only did I find their ghost stories to be quite compelling, I found the church's architecture and frescos to be absolutely breathtaking.

Dominique Doiron has been the executive director for the cultural center since 2009. He has no doubts about the place being haunted. Dominique had not heard anything about Saint Ann's being haunted prior to his arrival, but not long after he took the position one of the volunteers reported to him that she

The church's marble altar

would no longer work in the building alone. The volunteer had been downstairs in the Function Room, cleaning up around the stage, when she clearly heard a woman singing. The phantom voice seemed to be coming from the stage, but no one was there. When the volunteer discovered that she was the only person in the entire building, she became very scared and went home.

The chairman of the board, Wally Rathbun, was unable to meet with me the day I visited the center, so Dominique related a few stories about what the chairman has experienced. While working, Wally Rathbun sometimes thinks out loud when he could use something, like duct tape or a tool. Within moments of voicing his particular need, the item will show up as if someone were helping him. One of the funniest examples of this happened when Wally was helping mend costumes for a show, and he thought out loud that the dress he was working on could use "a big, gaudy flower." A few minutes later the chairman went to

Side by side comparison of two photographs taken by paranormal investigator Charles Reis in the Function Room. The photograph on the left appears to show a shadow figure standing in the kitchen. The picture on the right was taken shortly afterwards and does not show any dark form.

his office to retrieve something completely unrelated to the costuming job. When he opened up one of his cupboards he found a large, artificial flower, like the one he had just described, sitting on the middle shelf. Not only was the flower perfect for the dress, it had a pin in place on its back.

Another strange event Wally has mentioned is the sound of notes being played on the pipe organ. The organ is located on a balcony and can be easily observed from the floor of the church. No one has ever been seen near the keyboard when these notes have sounded, and there is nowhere for anyone to hide. What makes this even stranger is that it takes some considerable preparation to get this pipe organ ready to play. A person cannot play a note by pressing one of the keys unless the organ has been properly prepared. Dominique Doiron has heard single notes from the organ too, late in the day, when he has been alone in the building. His strangest moment with the organ was the time he looked inside one of its air baffles out of curiosity and found a bulky set of keys that he had lost a year earlier. He could find no explanation for how the keys had disappeared or how they could have ended up inside the pipe organ.

One of the board members who came to the center to meet with me was Jeannine Auger. She is a former parishioner and cares a great deal about the building's preservation. Jeannine's grandfather was one of those hardworking members of the French-Canadian community who helped to build Saint Ann's. For recognition of his contributions, he is immortalized in one of Guidi Nincheri's frescos on the church's ceiling. Jeannine has seen and heard enough to be convinced that there are ghosts wandering about the place. An experience she had with the pipe organ and its impossible notes confirmed for her that the spirits are past members of the congregation who feel as strongly about their church as she does. Prior to Jeannine hearing the pipe organ, a series of odd events happened. It was as if the building was reacting negatively to a theatrical event that was being staged at that time in the sanctuary. A local couple had made arrangements with the center to present six performances of a musical that they had written about vampires. Jeannine said, "A lot of things happened at that time, and I think that vampire show had a lot to do with it." Dominique then added, "It brought a lot of interesting people to the center that we haven't seen before, a lot of 'Goth.' I guess the best way to put it was the building didn't like the show."

An hour before the first performance, the fire alarms went off. The system has never had a false alarm in all the years the board members have been coming to the church. The fire department could find no fault in the system and no sign of a fire. During a performance on another night, a dressing screen fell on top of the leading man who was also the coauthor of the show. When this embarrassing moment took place on the stage, Dominique said he could hear "the radiators in the back chattering, almost like laughter." The heat had been turned off for some time when the stage furniture fell over, but even if it had been running, Dominique has never heard the heating system make a sound like it did at that precise moment.

Jeannine knew the building was not happy with the show

and its dark theme. She felt the morning after the last show would be a good time to talk to the ghosts and clear the air. Jeannine said, "I always talk to them." She told me about how her meeting with the spectral members of the board went. This is what she said happened: "I was working up here in the Chapel Room, and I knew that they were upset with the things that had been going on. I explained to them that I was sorry if they were upset about what happened. I told them, 'We're doing the best we can to raise money to keep the building open. I hope you're not too upset. Can you give me a sign?' From the organ came a note, another note, four or five times. Then my cell phone went off and it (the organ) stopped suddenly. I looked everywhere to see who could have done that because I know it came from the organ. It was my son who was calling my phone. I told him what happened and he just laughed!"

Jeannine has heard the pipe organ sound off on a few other occasions and so has her grandson. The two of them have also seen and heard some odd things in the Function Room. This large rental hall is where the volunteer said she had heard a woman singing. The phantom vocalist may also be the woman who has been heard crying in the ladies' room. Jeannine and her grandson have not encountered this female ghost, but they have seen a dark figure moving about the basement area. Their most unnerving moment downstairs was when the lid to a large trashcan flew off and thumped around in the kitchen. The shadow figure that Charles Reis photographed was also in the kitchen. If there is a ghost haunting the basement, then that might explain why Dominique Doiron and Wally Rathbun found bags of food sitting on the kitchen floor one morning. It looked to them as if someone had broken into the center during the night to steal food from the kitchen, but only got as far as placing what they wanted in bags. Something or someone must have scared them off, causing them to leave the food behind.

Spotlight On: Belcourt Castle Newport, Rhode Island

Belcourt Castle was built between 1891 and 1894 for Oliver Hazard Perry Belmont as a summer home. It was designed by Richard Morris Hunt who used Louis XIII's hunting lodge at Versailles as the model. Belmont's wife, Alva Vanderbilt, added to the original structure with examples of English, Italian, and German architecture. From 1933 to 1955, Belcourt (as it was originally called) passed through several owners and saw more neglect than restoration. The property was purchased in 1956 by the Tinney family of Cumberland, Rhode Island. The Tinneys conducted massive renovations to the whole building and made it a show place for their extensive collections of antiques. They are responsible for the mansion being renamed, Belcourt Castle. The house never had a reputation for being haunted

A helmet on one of theses suits of armor is believed to be haunted by the last knight to have worn it into battle.

in all the years prior to the Tinney's taking ownership. Harle Tinney is the last surviving member of the family since her husband's death in 2006. Mrs. Tinney believes that the ghosts of Belcourt Castle are spirits who are attached to certain items that her late husband, Donald, and his parents brought into the house. One of those items is a small, wooden statue of a monk.

When the statue first came into the Tinneys' possession they placed it on display at their previous home. That was the first time they caught sight of the shadowy figure which seems to be linked to the wooden monk. Two weeks after the statue was brought to Belcourt Castle, the dark figure was spotted again. Since then it has been seen no fewer than five times and always within the vicinity of the statue. Donald and Harle Tinney saw the ghost in the Great Hall when the statue was displayed there on a stand by the door to the ladies' room. At first, they both thought the figure was Donald's father. However, as the figure opened the door to the restroom the couple could clearly see it was not Mr. Tinney. What also struck them was the fact that the door, which always creaked loudly, made no sound on its hinges. Donald and Harle found no one in the small room when they checked.

The wooden monk is now kept in the Chapel Room on the first floor. It was moved there after a psychic told the Tinneys that the entity attached to the little monk wanted it placed there. That hasn't stopped the dark shade from making an appearance from time to time. The most recent sighting was on July 7, 2007, at seven o'clock in the evening. Belcourt Castle was playing host to a wedding when Harle Tinney saw what she thought was a guest heading in the wrong direction. She moved after the figure as it went into the foyer, but as she reached the spot she found no one there.

The Gothic Ballroom located on the second floor has had its share of unsettling moments as well. One night in the mid-1990s, Harle Tinney heard three bloodcurdling screams while standing in the middle of the darkened ballroom. Her two dogs reacted to the screaming, but were far too afraid to enter the room. There is an impressive collection of knights' armor on exhibit in this room. The suits of armor are all excellent reproductions, except for one helmet which is known to be authentic and does show a battle scar. It is believed the knight who once wore the helmet haunts the armor and what Harle Tinney heard that evening were his death screams.

The late Donald Tinney heard the sound of a party in progress inside the ballroom. It was late in the evening and the house was very still. When he went to investigate the phantom gathering, the family cat came along with him. It seemed to be well aware of the music and chatter. The cat started growling and the fur on its back and tail stood up when the two of them reached the ballroom. The sound then faded away into nothingness as Donald Tinney opened the doors to the room. This ghostly encounter is believed to have been a trace haunting of a happier moment in the home's history, possibly from the Gilded Age.

In 1996 a woman who was a guest at a private party being held on the first floor came upstairs to use the ladies' room that is located in Ruth Tinney's (Donald's mother) old bedroom. Most of the room is roped off, leaving only the bathroom accessible to the public. As the guest entered the room she noticed there was a lady sitting at Ruth Tinney's desk. The guest addressed the lady and informed her that no one was allowed behind the ropes. The mysterious lady ignored the woman and her warning. Unnerved by this, the guest went to alert security of the intrusion. A guard was standing close by and lost no time getting to the bedroom. The lady was gone without a trace. No one could have left the room without being seen and there was no place for anyone to hide. When Harle Tinney heard the guest's description of the lady it was a perfect match for her late mother-in-law. That day was also the one-year anniversary of

Spotlight On: Belcourt Castle
(continued)

Ruth Tinney's death. Twice in 2010, the bedspread on Ruth Tinney's bed was seen to be disturbed. A young Englishwoman taking a tour of Belcourt Castle told Harle Tinney that she had witnessed the bedspread move as if someone was getting up off the bed. In July of that same year, Harle Tinney took a couple on a tour of the house and while they were in the bedroom she mentioned her late mother-in-law. The bedspread, as if on cue, flew right off the bed and landed several feet away on the floor. All Harle Tinney could do was say, "Hi Mom!"

I spoke with Ken and Dave DeCosta, the father and son co-founders of the Rhode Island Society for the Examination of Unusual Phenomena (R.I.S.E.U.P.). Their paranormal team has been allowed into Belcourt Castle to conduct investigations and public ghost hunts. They told me that they have not seen or caught any of the ghosts on camera, but they have recorded examples of electronic voice phenomenon (EVP) throughout the property. Ken and Dave told me the EVPs that were recorded seem to be of a personal nature, so out of respect for the Tinney family they have declined to give me any further details on what the spirit voices said. The most interesting moment caught by R.I.S.E.U.P. on video was a session involving two electromagnetic field (EMF) meters. A member of the team asked if any spirit present could make the lights flash on one of the meters. After the lights on one of the meters flashed on and off, they asked if the spirit could do the same with the other EMF meter lying nearby on the same table. That meter's lights flashed on and off while the first meter's lights stayed off. The team continued asking the spirit to please go back and forth between the two meters and the lights flashed on and off as requested. All cell phones were switched off and no other electromagnetic interference could be found within the room.

CHAPTER 12

Tavern on Main
CHEPACHET, RHODE ISLAND

The Tavern on Main (aka The Stagecoach Tavern) could quite possibly be the most haunted business in Rhode Island.

INNS AND TAVERNS WERE ESSENTIAL ESTAB-LISHMENTS along the main streets and post roads in every town, village, and hamlet for hundreds of years. Travel was nothing like it is today. Whether it was on horseback, by stagecoach, or on foot, getting from one town to the next was long, hard and tiring for both man and beast. Weary from their journey, folks would need a place to get out of the elements, take food and drink, as well as rest, water, and feed their horses. In 1800 a man named Cyrus Cooke established an inn on Main Street

A shadowy figure has been spotted around this booth. Customers have also reported seeing items move on the table while they were seated here.

in Chepachet, Rhode Island. Sometime before the mid 1800s it became the Jedediah Sprague Tavern. Sprague's Hotel, as it was also called, would be the central location for one of the most important moments in Rhode Island's history.

Thomas Dorr was a lawyer who led a suffrage movement against unfair laws regulating the rights of free men to vote in the Union's smallest state. The original charter (written in 1663) held that only men who owned land could vote. By the time of the Industrial Revolution, most men lived and worked in the cities and did not own land. This made 60 percent of the state's population ineligible to vote. Dorr created the People's Convention to give the disenfranchised a party to represent them. An election was held in April of 1842, and Thomas Dorr won the seat of Governor. Dorr's opposition, the Law and Order Party, returned incumbent Governor Samuel Ward King to office two days later. Dorr was labeled an outlaw and had a $5,000 bounty placed on him.

After a failed attempt to get President John Tyler involved, Dorr returned home in late June and made the Jedediah Sprague Tavern his headquarters. Sprague was a "Dorrite" and served his governor as military adviser. When Dorr insisted the Rhode Island General Assembly convene at the tavern on July Fourth of that year, King sent twenty-five hundred troops to crush the rebellion. Thomas Dorr knew his militia could not win against those numbers and ordered his men to go back to their homes. He then fled the state. Governor King's men punished Sprague by staying at his tavern for the remainder of summer, eating and drinking all they wanted without ever paying.

The old building has gone through many owners in the twentieth century. It has been an apartment house, a pool hall, and a pub. For about the last twenty-five years it has been serving as a restaurant. Formally named the Stagecoach Tavern, the Tavern on Main is known locally as a good place to meet friends for drinks and to have a good meal. Its exposed post-and-beam construction made from handhewn lumber creates a warm and inviting atmosphere. It seems the location's long and varied history has also added to its haunted reputation. The building's most active areas for paranormal activity are the Tap Room (bar), the downstairs dining room, and the upstairs dining room, referred to as the Dorr Ballroom. Starting at the bar, here are some of the most unusual moments that have occurred at the tavern.

The Tap Room is where the most horrific moment in the tavern's history took place. Yes, all bars do have spirits, and drinking them can impair one's judgment, but most of the witnesses to these events have been employees who absolutely do not drink on duty. In the early 1970s, a deranged man who could not accept the end of a relationship walked into the bar with a handgun and shot his ex-girlfriend to death. Such sudden and violent deaths are believed to be the catalyst for hauntings. It is possible the woman's restless spirit may be responsible for some of the shocking things that have been seen and heard in the bar since her murder. A patron named Steve, who is described as a "biker dude," was making loud comments one night about how ridiculous it was that people thought the place was haunted. Right as he was declaring his disbelief in ghosts, the large television set above and behind him fell off of its shelf, missing him by inches. There was no explanation for how the TV could have fallen. Witnesses said it didn't slide; the set looked like it lifted up and off before it fell to the floor. It is back up on its shelf, still working fine, and it hasn't moved an inch ever since.

Debra Marks has worked at the tavern since 1997. Debra says, "People always ask me, 'Have you seen a ghost?'" Her answer to their question is, "If I ever see a ghost, you won't see me! I'm not working here if I see a ghost!" Debra has experienced some strange things. There was the Sunday morning when she went to unlock the front door and was disappointed to find the candy dish was empty. Debra recalls, "I really wanted a mint." A brief moment later, after unlocking the door, there were about a dozen mints sitting in the dish. Debra tries to ignore odd occurrences, such as lights turning on and off. Hearing a voice call her by name when no one was around, she admits, was a little unsettling. But there were two nights in the Tap Room that really made her feel uneasy.

In August 2010, Debra was closing the place up with a fellow employee named Derrick. It was around one a.m., and there were no customers left in the building—it was just the two of them. The Tap Room was quiet, with no radio or TV on. Debra froze when she heard the sink in the ladies' room turn on full blast. Her first thought was that someone was hiding in there. She cautiously approached the door to the washroom and called out, "Derrick?" Derrick then came into the Tap Room through a doorway behind the bar; he wasn't the one using the water.

The ghost of the little boy haunts the ladies' room.

When Derrick pushed open the door to the ladies' room, he found the sink on at full stream, with no one in there. Two weeks later, Debra and Derrick were once again cleaning up at closing time. At about one a.m., they heard a scream from inside the men's room. "It was a weird, high-pitched scream," says Debra. "We have apartments upstairs, so I was trying to rationalize. But it was coming from the men's bathroom." They could find no source for the scream. There have been other reports of a scream heard in this part of the building as well.

The downstairs dining room seems to be the realm of three ghosts. In the front corner booth, by the windows, employees and patrons have heard the sound of a woman sobbing. There are stories of people seeing her sad ghost seated in the corner, wearing a nineteenth-century-style dress. Customers dining in the booth have had their utensils disappear, and waitresses have found the place settings in a condition that looked like someone had pushed them with a swipe of their hand. What makes this haunting somewhat touching is the fact that the reports are more frequent around Saint Valentine's Day.

The second ghost known to haunt the downstairs dining room is that of a little boy who seems to be aware of his surroundings and those who have encountered him. He is described as being no more than six years of age, wearing breeches, and a white shirt with a wide, round collar. He is also described as friendly, giving those who have seen him a warm smile before he disappears. One witness to this spirit told me she didn't know of the Tavern on Main's haunted reputation before having lunch there one afternoon. As she was enjoying her meal, she looked up to see a little boy wearing clothes from the early 1900s. He was standing a few feet from the table and looking right at her. The lady thought the child was part of some historical reenactment in town that she was unaware of. She smiled at him and said, "Hello." The boy smiled back, and as he turned to move away, he vanished. When the lady inquired about the boy in period costume she was informed that there were no reenactors in town that day. She had probably seen the tavern's "little boy," and she was told not to worry.

Debra Marks told me she had a friend who stopped by the tavern one evening with his three-and-a-half-year-old daughter to say hello and pick up an order of food to go. While waiting for his order, he took his daughter to the ladies' room, located off of the downstairs dining room. This small washroom has only one door and no windows. The man stood outside the door and kept an ear on his young daughter. When he heard the girl talking and giggling, he pushed the door open a crack and asked if she was all done. She answered back, "I'm playing with the little boy." The father then pushed the door all the way open and saw his child conversing with empty air. Her dad called her to come out, and she started waving good-bye to her invisible friend. "Daddy, say bye-bye," she told her father. Later that night, the man saw Debra after she got home from work and told her what had happened. He confessed to Debra, "I was never so scared in all my life."

The third ghost to be encountered downstairs is a shadowy figure, believed to be a man. A video camera left running in the dining room by a ghosthunter in 2005 may have caught this ghost. The video appears to show a strange, gray distortion get up from one of the booths and move towards the back door. In June of 2010, employee Stacey Perreault was asked by a group of women to take a photograph of them. As Stacey was about to take aim with their camera, she saw a dark, man-shaped shadow move along the wall towards the back door. A wall-mounted light went off as the form moved by it, but then came back on as soon as the shadow had passed. One of the women looked right at Ms. Perreault and asked, "Did you see that?"

In the Dorr Ballroom there have been reports of a man in Colonial-era garb standing by the top of the front staircase. One afternoon an employee went to investigate a strange flapping sound and discovered that there were drink coasters scattered all over the stairs. The coasters had been stacked on a table in the ballroom, close to the staircase. On the night of October 30, 2007, I was sitting in about the same spot where the drink coasters had been. My back was about a foot and a half away from a low wall that separates the dining area from the staircase. An antique washboard was sitting as a decoration on the ledge that runs along the top of the low wall. I suddenly heard a quick shuffling sound behind me, but before I could react, the heavy washboard hit me on the left shoulder and grazed the side of my head as it continued across the table and on to the floor. A group of young women, who were sitting at a table to my right, told me they saw the washboard spin off of the shelf, apparently by itself. None of us there that night could explain how this could have happened. The Tavern on Main could quite possibly be the most haunted business in all of Rhode Island.

Spotlight On:
The Village of Chepachet
Glocester, Rhode Island

Chepachet is one of the oldest settlements in northwestern Rhode Island. In the eighteenth and nineteenth centuries, Chepachet was a bustling center of business and government. It is situated at the crossings of Routes 44 and 102, which were two of the state's original turnpikes. This busy little village still contains many of its historic homes and buildings, making it a popular destination for people to visit and sightsee. There are also small shops and antique stores to browse. The Brown and Hopkins Store, located on Main Street, is the nation's oldest continuously running general store.

Over the years, I have learned that this attractive village and the surrounding area are very haunted. It seems that one can't throw a stone there without hitting a place that contains a ghost or two.

Acotes Hill Cemetery

As a paranormal researcher, it makes sense to me. A place as rich in history as Chepachet, with so many well-preserved sites, would likely make an excellent conduit for psychical phenomena.

Starting on the east side of the village (on Route 44 West), the first haunted site is Acote's Hill. This hill was named after a half-breed peddler named Acote. The itinerant salesman was killed at a local hotel and buried on the west side of the hill in an unmarked grave in the early 1800s. Since the mid-1800s, it has been known as Acote's Hill Cemetery. Locals and visitors to the cemetery have reported seeing the ghosts of men in military garb in the older (west) part of the burial ground. During the Dorr Rebellion of 1842, Governor Dorr's men had constructed a defensible position on the hilltop, but no blood was ever shed. There are many military veterans buried there, so it is difficult to give an identity to these ghostly soldiers.

A waitress at the Tavern on Main told me about a ghost she and her family lived with in a house located on the opposite side of Route 44 from Acote's Hill. The ghost is that of a pretty, young girl with long, blond banana curls. There was nothing sinister about the little wraith, but there was one room in the house where the waitress's husband could not enter without books and other objects flying off the shelves. After they relocated elsewhere, an acquaintance of the waitress moved into the home, not knowing anything about the paranormal activity. This second family reported seeing the same little girl as well.

Continue traveling west on Route 44 and pass the Tavern on Main. On the left-hand side of the road stands the Chepachet fire station. There are stories about phantom footsteps and sounds heard in the building from time to time. A friend of mine, Wendy Gill, told me her son-in-law was once stationed there, and he too heard stories from other firefighters that the building was haunted. One end of the building appears to be built over an old mill channel. The haunting may have something to do with a former structure that stood there, rather than the fire station.

Spotlight On:
The Village of Chepachet
(continued)

Across the street from the station is the Old Stone Mill antiques store. The building was constructed in 1814 and was originally used as a store. Additions were made to the property when it was converted into a textile mill. A fire later destroyed all but the original stone building. The current owner is Debra McCarron. On my first visit to her antiques shop I came right out and asked her if she had ever experienced anything strange in the old stone building. She laughed as she answered, "Yes!" Before moving the business into the building, she and her husband had to do a lot of cleaning and preparation. They performed most of this work late in the evening. Debra said she would often hear the sound of children laughing and running around on the second floor. Her husband arrived alone one night to do some renovations and found the heavy wooden door locked from the inside by a large iron eyehook. After forcing the door open, he looked around for any evidence that someone may have been in the building and had locked the door to prevent being caught in the act. No signs of illegal entry were found. Debra told me she gets along with her ghosts and hasn't had any problems herself.

Cross over the river to the next building on the right, the oldest in Chepachet. It is currently The Town Trader antiques store. It is made up of five separate buildings dating from the 1690s to the 1980s. It has served as a trading post, a boarding house, a diner, and a hardware store as well as a private residence. The current owners, Eileen and Charlie, have been there for more than six years. They were told that the previous owner had mentioned seeing "things" during his time in the building. Charlie told me that while doing repair work to the building's interior he occasionally saw a white blur out of the corner of his eye. They have seen furniture move, and their cat sometimes reacts to "something" that no on else can see. The activity seems to kick up whenever the attic is disturbed.

There is another ghost that haunts a private apartment near the traffic lights. My friend Wendy knows a young woman who once lived in the old house, and she told Wendy and her daughter that she saw a man in eighteenth-century clothing standing at the foot of her bed late one night. The next tenant to live there, who was not told of this encounter, later reported seeing the same apparition.

I know of a few other haunted homes in the area, but I will conclude with a ghost that was seen on Reservoir Road, which is located a short distance outside the village, directly off of Route 44 (West). An elderly couple I met at the Tavern on Main told me about a ghost they saw one afternoon while driving home on Reservoir Road. It was a gray, rainy day, but visibility was still good. As they were traveling down the road, a man wearing a cape materialized out of thin air in the middle of the road. The husband told me this strange man was somewhat transparent and seemed to be running in the same direction as the car. The husband drove right through the running man and immediately stopped the car. He felt no impact against the car and there was no body in the road. The husband said to me, "If she (his wife) had come home and told me that story, I would have thought she was nuts. But I was driving and I saw him. I now believe in ghosts!"

CHAPTER 13

Stillwater Antiques

GREENVILLE, RHODE ISLAND

Stillwater Antiques is located in the oldest section of the Greenville Mill.

GREENVILLE IS A SMALL VILLAGE located along Route 44 in the town of Smithfield, Rhode Island. Joshua Windsor became the first European to settle in the area when he built a mill here in 1685. The village didn't have an official name until 1785. It was then named Greenville in honor of Major-General Nathanael Greene, the Rhode Island-born patriot who served with great distinction during the War of Independence. Besides being a suitable location to build water-powered mills, the early settlers found the soil and terrain in Greenville to be ideal for cultivating apples. This part of Smithfield has been called "Apple

Valley" for many years now. A small number of family orchards still survive today and continue to produce some of the finest apples available in southern New England.

Only two of Greenville's mills remain standing. They were both built during the American Industrial Revolution as textile factories. In 1990 the former Greenville Manufacturing Company, located on Austin Avenue, was converted into private apartments. The Greenville Finishing Company on Putnam Pike came to an end in 1970. Since then, the old building (referred to as the Greenville Mill) has housed a number of small businesses. The oldest section of the property dates back to the early 1830s. It was known then as the Pooke & Steere Woolen Mill. In 1908 the business was identified as The Greenville Woolen Mill by a newspaper reporting on the senseless murder of Mary Eddy. The unfortunate young woman had been an employee at the mill and was killed for her week's pay. I found out about this all-but-forgotten crime from a local historian and writer, Jim Ignasher. Not too long after Jim shared this story with me, I learned of a suicide and two haunts that were brought about by Mary Eddy's murder.

The first ghostly tale came up during a conversation I had with a former Greenville resident, Ed Robinson. We were discussing haunted places in the town of Smithfield when Ed, who had no prior knowledge of Jim Ignasher's research into the Eddy case, volunteered a family ghost story involving the murdered girl who worked at the Greenville Mill. Ed remembered his aunt telling him many years ago about the ghost of a former handyman that haunts their family's original homestead in Greenville. Ed's aunt said the man had lived in the house and kept a room in the attic. He was in love with a young woman who worked at the nearby Greenville Mill and they were engaged to be married. When his fiancée was robbed and killed on her way home from the mill, the handyman, overwrought with grief,

hung himself in the attic stairway. I already knew of this historic home and its haunted reputation, but I was unaware of
the facts behind the tragic suicide. The current homeowner has
informed me that the ghost is indeed still active and makes his
presence known from time to time.

A short time after my talk with Ed Robinson, I was inter-
viewing a Greenville business owner about the ghosts that haunt
her establishment. Kimberly Hopkins operates her custom hat
shop, Hopkins Millinery, in one of the oldest surviving houses
in the village, and the property does appear to be haunted.
While we were talking about local ghosts, Kimberly mentioned
that her late grandfather, Arthur Paine, worked for ten years at
The Greenville Finishing Company as a night watchman. She
recalled Grandpa Paine telling her about a woman in white that
walks the overgrown road that used to run all the way from Putnam Pike (RT 44) to Austin Avenue. He told Kimberly the specter was that of a murdered girl who was attacked and robbed on
her way home from the mill. Mary Eddy received a horrific blow
to the back of her head while walking home from the textile factory along Pig Road on January 3, 1908. The abandoned road is
now referred to as Mapleville Road. It is the first right turn after
the Greenville Mill if one is traveling west on Route 44. The
road is paved for only a few hundred yards before it ends at a
guardrail and small parking area for the Cascade Brook Conser-
vation Area. Cascade Brook offers public walking trails that parallel part of the overgrown road where Ms. Eddy was assaulted
and is said to haunt.

Kimberly Hopkins telephoned me a little while after my visit
to her hat shop and suggested that I visit the Greenville Mill. She
had been told the place had a strange reputation. I also received a
phone call from Jim Ignasher to tell me he had heard the antiques
center at the mill was thought to be haunted. I thanked them
both for their valuable input and set out for the mill.

When I went to Stillwater Antiques and asked the owners if they felt the building was haunted, they didn't hesitate
in answering, "Yes." The Rossi family purchased the business
(formerly The Greenville Antique Center) in August 2010. They
had been renting dealer space in the old mill for fourteen years,
so when the original owners put the business up for sale, the
Rossis decided to take a shot at running the place. In all the
years Jean Rossi and her husband were renting space as dealers, she never heard anyone say anything about the mill being
haunted. It wasn't until they took over and started rearranging things that Jean and her son, Mike, began to feel there was
something unusual about the building.

The Rossis describe the paranormal activity in their antique
center as fleeting. Mike told me, "You see it out of the corner of
your eye, in your peripheral vision." The activity seems to occur
mostly in the evening when the building is quiet. I asked Mike
to tell me about the things he has experienced while closing at
night. He told me he has heard sounds that just don't belong
there, sounds that cannot be traced back to a likely source. Mike
said, "They're not normal noises; they're unsettling." After a
short pause he added, "I've heard a moan. You've got to hear it.
It has heaviness to it." Mike has also detected the sound of feet
scuffing on the floor near the front counter.

One evening in November 2010, Jean Rossi heard phantom
footsteps in the same location. It was around seven o'clock and
she was alone in the quiet building. Jean said, "I had walked
across the floor down here (by the front counter) and I could hear
my own footsteps. When I stopped to look at a piece of paper,
I could hear steps following me. I counted thirteen." Jean was
locked out of her office on three consecutive days in February
2011. She leaves her office open while spending most of the day
working out front at the counter. Three afternoons in a row, she
found the door closed and locked from the inside. Jean assured

me that there was no way she could have accidently or absent-mindedly shut and locked the door. It seemed deliberate each time it happened. The door locked only when Jean had left her keys in the office and Mike (with his set of keys) was elsewhere on the property. She is certain the door was locked by one of the ghosts that haunt the second floor. The former factory floor now holds over two hundred dealer stalls, which offer every-thing from antique furniture to kitschy collectibles. However, the ghosts seem to prefer the front half of the building (which is the oldest section), especially the second floor. One evening at closing time, Jean Rossi caught sight of a partial apparition near the foot of the wide stairway that leads from the dealers' area to the second floor. From what little Jean could make out, she thinks it was a man in a uniform.

One of the phantoms Mike Rossi has perceived out of the corner of his eye stands at the top of the stairs. It is a stern look-ing woman wearing a long, old-fashioned dress. The second floor is currently used for storage and is closed to the public. Mike tries to avoid going up there if he can. As he showed me around the second floor, Mike told me, "It's almost a suffocat-ing feeling; it's that uncomfortable to come up here sometimes. It feels like there's a banquet going on up here some nights. But there's one (spirit) up here that is king; he's the boss." His mother agrees and believes that she has seen this ghost watch-ing her. While working on the second floor, Jean has seen a man wearing blue work pants and a white T-shirt. Every time Jean has seen this man he has been standing off to the side, almost out of her line of sight. He has an assertive air about him, and she gets the strong feeling he worked with machin-ery. Jean thinks he is a misogynist and resents her being in his domain. She has dealt with his intimidating presence by simply ignoring him. This is why Jean is sure he's the one responsible for locking the office door.

The second floor of the mill is haunted by a stern, male spirit.

I was able to walk through the building at night with my good friend and colleague, Pamela Patalano, who is a very gifted psychic. She has had remarkably accurate hits at many of the locations we have investigated together. Without knowing anything about the Rossis' own personal experiences, Pam detected the activity on the second floor and had some of the same impressions as Mike and Jean. She sensed a stern woman at the top of the stairs and a rotund man who watches over the factory floor. Pam not only picked up on the man in the blue pants and white T-shirt, she pointed to the exact spot where Jean Rossi has seen him most often. Pam also felt the same negative vibes that Mike Rossi gets whenever he's around the old elevator shaft. She could see a confused man hanging around there, as if he was simpleminded when he was alive. His name wasn't clear to Pam, but she felt his first name sounded something like Ernest or Ernie.

I found this interesting later when Jim Ignasher reminded me that Mary Eddy's killer was named Earl Jacques. Jacques was also employed at the mill. He crushed her skull with a wooden dowel used to stir the dye vats. At his trial, Jacques's mother claimed he wasn't "right in the head" and that her son couldn't understand the gravity of the crime he had committed. Is it possible that Mary Eddy's pathetic murderer haunts the mill while her ghost walks the overgrown road, and her fiancé's spirit stays grounded to the site of his lonely suicide?

During the day, Stillwater Antiques is a great place to walk around in and brose. Each dealer stall is like a miniature museum, and the old mill building is an interesting piece of history all on its own. Pamela Patalano and the Rossis agree that the ghosts at the Greenville Mill seem very territorial. The mill is their domain, and when the sun sets they let it be known. Mike Rossi will never forget the night when the lights upstairs were turned back on as he was leaving. Ever since that happened, he doesn't like to look back at the building after closing. Mike said, "I lock the doors at night, and I can feel them watching me as I walk to my car."

Spotlight On: Historic Cemetery Number Two
West Greenwich, Rhode Island

At the intersection of Plain Road and Plain Meeting House Road in West Greenwich, Rhode Island, stands an old Baptist church (meetinghouse) and behind it lies its graveyard. The meetinghouse is rarely used, but the cemetery is still receiving members of the community who have departed this world. Unfortunately, it also receives a lot of disrespectful attention from foolish teenagers who visit the site because they have heard that a vampire is buried there. The vandalism that has resulted from their bad behavior is inexcusable.

As I have been led to understand, the trouble all started sometime in the late 1970s when a school teacher told a group of students the story of Mercy Brown, the Rhode Island vampire. Apparently the teacher's knowledge of Mercy's tale was greatly inaccurate, including the whereabouts of her grave and her name. When some teenagers later discovered the gravestone of a nineteen-year-old girl in the graveyard of the West Greenwich Baptist Church

The old Baptist Church on Plain Meeting House Road. Its graveyard is haunted by the ghost of Nellie Vaughn.

with a seemingly cryptic epitaph, word got around that the vampire's grave had been found.

The grave was in fact that of Nellie Vaughn who died in 1889 of pneumonia, not tuberculosis like the rest of the alleged New England vampires. Vaughn was originally buried on property at her family's home. She was then removed and brought to the Baptist cemetery for reburial in consecrated ground. Her epitaph read, "I am waiting and watching for you." This was not an uncommon message to be carved into a gravestone in the nineteenth century. It simply means the departed would be keeping an eye on loved ones while waiting for them in Heaven.

I say her epitaph "read" because her stone no longer stands above her grave. After being chipped and broken by souvenir hunters, it was removed altogether. One story says it was stolen, and another says it was taken by the town for safekeeping. An additional falsehood claims that nothing will grow on her sunken grave. The reason for that was somebody tried to dig up her grave several years ago and the disturbed ground took some time to settle and allow for vegetation to take root. I have been to her grave recently and it is now covered in grass, clover, and moss. Misguided youths continue to visit the cemetery and seek out Nellie Vaughn's grave. They perform black magic rituals and try to communicate with dark forces. Worst of all, they knock over gravestones and have attempted to break into tombs. This might explain the ghost stories that have come from the cemetery in the last twenty or so years. People have reported seeing a strange young woman in a white dress near the location of Nellie Vaughn's grave. It is believed she is not happy with the state of her final resting place.

All the stories I have heard about Nellie Vaughn's ghost have been secondhand and seem to be nothing more than fanciful additions to the myth. However, I was given one account by an eyewitness that left me believing there could truly be something to the haunting.

A firefighter in my hometown overheard me talking to a waitress about ghosts. He joined in on the conversation and told me he had seen the ghost of the vampire in West Greenwich. I politely explained to him that Nellie Vaughn was misidentified as one of New England's vampires and his reaction was, "Well, maybe she wasn't a vampire, but I saw her ghost with my own eyes." He went on to explain that he, his brother, and two cousins went to the cemetery one night in 1982 to check out the grave that their friends had been talking about. He said as his cousin pulled the car into the dirt parking lot next to the meetinghouse they all caught sight of someone moving around by the back wall of the graveyard. It looked like a woman in a white dress. Because they were skeptical about the whole story, they thought someone must be playing a prank. By the time they got out of the car and began walking into the cemetery, the woman was nowhere to be seen. The meetinghouse and cemetery are in an isolated spot with thick woods all around. The stone wall is fairly wide too, so it was hard for them to understand where the woman could have gone.

The small party reached the back of the cemetery and began to look around for the woman. The firefighter assured me that he and the others had not been drinking or taking drugs. He wished they had because it would have explained the terrifying sight that appeared out of nowhere. He told me they had turned around to continue walking about, and there before them was a woman, glowing white and hovering a few inches off the ground. He confessed that the four of them screamed like little girls and ran as fast as they could back to his cousin's car.

When they reached the parking lot the four of them jumped in the car. He said his cousin's car ran great and always started on the first turn of the key, but not on that night. It took more than a couple of tries to get the engine to start, and the whole time they could see the ghostly woman hovering on the path leading to the cemetery gate. When the car finally started up, his cousin slammed it into reverse and then gunned out of the parking lot. The firefighter told me he could still recall the sound of the car's hubcaps coming off and rolling away as they sped off on the unpaved gravel. He finished his tale by saying he now believes in ghosts and never doubts any stories about the paranormal.

Spotlight On: Moosup Valley
Foster, Rhode Island

In the southwest corner of the town of Foster, Rhode Island, sits the tiny, quaint hamlet of Moosup Valley. This quiet rural area was established in 1705 and is listed on the National Register of Historic Places. Consisting of only a few homesteads and open fields, the main points of interest are the Foster Country Club and the Dyer Woods Nudist Colony. At the heart of the hamlet (located on Moosup Valley Road) is the Tyler Free Library, the Moosup Valley Congregational Church, Grange Hall, and Tyler Cemetery. It is quite the slice of New England charm—in the daylight.

The master of horror, H. P. Lovecraft, lived here in his early childhood. Lovecraft said of Moosup Valley, "I haunted it in infancy." His family's home was located on Johnson Road, but, unfortunately, it burned down many years ago. Another resident of the area with a macabre reputation was Nancy Young, one of Rhode Island's "vampires." She died April 6, 1827, of tuberculosis, and not long afterwards her brothers and sisters became ill with the dreaded disease. When her siblings began talking about Nancy visiting them late at night, their parents and neighbors feared the worst: Nancy had become a vampire. Her grave was opened up and her body was set on fire. The Young children were made to breath in the smoke in order to rid themselves of the vampire's curse. Sadly, all of them died and were buried alongside their sister Nancy.

Moosup Valley Road is haunted by a phantom known as the "Grange Hall Ghost." The apparition is said to be a man dressed in work clothes and carrying a shovel over his shoulder. The only documented sighting of this ghost appeared in an edition of the *Moosup Valley Moose*, a local paper that once covered events in the town of Foster. A former resident named Alfred C. Andrews had written a letter to the paper shortly after visiting the town for the

Labor Day clambake. Andrews told the paper that every time he returned to Moosup Valley he was reminded of something strange that had happened to him when he lived there in the 1960s.

Andrews's strange tale took place over a period of about five years and involved three sightings of a weird figure along Moosup Valley Road he had late at night. All three encounters took place during the fall season, around 11:30 p.m., as he was driving home from work. The first encounter happened as Andrews crossed over the Moosup Valley Bridge, just before the Tyler Cemetery. He noticed a middle-aged man in work clothes walking past the cemetery towards the bridge. This odd character was over his shoulder carrying a shovel with a badly broken blade. Andrews thought it very strange that this man didn't react to the car's headlights. The man didn't blink or look away; he stared straight ahead and kept on walking. When Andrews drove past the man he looked in his rearview mirror, but couldn't see him anywhere.

About two years later, he saw the strange man with the shovel again. It was at the same time at night on October 17. He recalled the date because it was his daughter's birthday. This time Andrews spotted him on the bridge, sitting still and staring straight ahead. Andrews wrote, "I don't mind telling you that it sent a chill up my spine." Again, he glanced in the rearview mirror and the mysterious man was gone. From that point on, Andrews was very nervous about driving through Moosup Valley at night.

The third and last time he saw the man was about three years later. On that night the man with the broken shovel was standing in front of the Grange Hall, which is located beyond the cemetery and across from the church. Andrews worked up the courage to slow down and take a good look at him. The man was standing very still and, as usual, staring straight ahead. Andrews wrote, "He seemed to be very tired, and he seemed like he was either resting or waiting for something. I forced myself to look directly into his face as I drove by and suddenly became very frightened by that deep stare and blank expression. As I drove past I quickly looked in my rearview mirror, and, once again, the figure had disappeared."

A local woman, Pat Morgan, told me that she had heard the ghost is also seen on nearby Gold Mine Road. The road was named after a failed gold mining operation in the early 1900s. Perhaps the Grange Hall Ghost is a former miner who traveled that route every day to work at the mine.

I have visited Moosup Valley Road many times. In the daytime it is an attractive place, but at night it feels different. There are few lights along the road, and when the local inhabitants settle down for the night the area becomes absolutely still. When I asked one of the ladies who works at the Tyler Free Library if she had ever seen or heard anything unusual she said, "No, but when it gets dark early, and I have to close the library alone, I lock the door and get to my car as quick as I can."

I have captured some strange anomalies while ghosthunting on the road. A photograph I took of the church in daylight with a 35mm camera shows a strange black and gray shape on the edge of the picture. A photo technician examined the negative and could find no explanation for the shadow-like shape. The technician told me it was not a problem with the camera, the film, or the development process. Whatever it was appeared between the camera and the church and was not an error (like my thumb) against the camera's lens. I also caught a bizarre object on infrared video. The video was shot on a September night in 2007, under a full moon, at about 11:30. I saw nothing at the moment it was recorded, but I did feel somewhat uneasy at the time. When the video is advanced one frame at a time, the object looks like a piece of translucent fabric swirling through the night air. This twisting shape appears to leave the ground from directly behind me and move quickly into the cemetery right at the moment I turned around with my video camera in hand.

My favorite piece of "evidence" captured on Moosup Valley Road is an example of electronic voice phenomenon (EVP) that was recorded by Kyle Bell of Hampden Paranormal Society. Kyle and I were standing in front of the Grange Hall one night in early October 2009. He had recently purchased an electromagnetic field detector (EMF meter) and wanted to try it out in a haunted location. Kyle turned on his digital audio recorder and the EMF meter and began speaking to the Grange Hall Ghost. He spoke in a polite tone, telling the spirit that it could communicate with us by making the lights light up on the device in his hand. Nothing happened. The following day, Kyle sent me a clip from the audio recording made at the moment he politely explained the EMF meter to the ghost. A soft, whispery voice responded with, "So?" I guess if one is a ghost with a broken shovel and broken dreams of striking gold, a college kid with a fancy contraption doesn't hold much interest.

The Moosup Valley Grange Hall. This photograph was taken the night Kyle Bell recorded the EVP of a man saying, "So?"

CHAPTER 14

Hopkins Mills
FOSTER, RHODE ISLAND

The ghost of Aunt Lonnie Davis has been seen sitting on the wall of this cemetery.

FOSTER, RHODE ISLAND, was incorporated in 1781 when it separated from the town of Scituate. Throughout the nineteenth and early twentieth centuries, Foster was considered by many Rhode Islanders to be the "Wild West." The town had a nefarious reputation for being inhabited by hard-living people who worked in grist and saw mills, milked cows, and maintained charcoal pits. I have seen newspaper stories from this time period where the reporters made derogatory remarks about the town and its inhabitants. One quote from 1899 reads, "It would be difficult to imagine a more apparently uncivilized region in a civilized state. Houses are few and generally far apart. Everywhere there is wooded land and rocks and hills." Those last two points are still true today. The houses are few and far between, and the rocky hills are covered with trees. Foster is a quiet, rural community with a population of less than five thousand. I have spoken with many town residents over the years, and I found them all to be friendly and very helpful. It is safe to say the region is now quite civilized. All year round Foster is a great place to take a slow drive through. The unspoiled forests, historic buildings, farms, and Colonial-era cemeteries make great photo opportunities, especially in the fall when the foliage begins to turn color. It is also a very haunted place. I have found through research and interviews that this small, quiet town has a history of murder, suicide, foul crimes, and witchcraft. Perhaps the area's relatively unchanged and unspoiled environment holds more than just natural beauty. Some of the people I have talked to tell me there are places in Foster that retain some dark shades from the town's past. The most haunted area in the town is the hamlet of Hopkins Mills. It was one of the original settlements in this part of the state, and in 1999 it was placed on the National Register of Historic Places. The name comes from Ezekiel Hopkins, the first man to settle in Foster and the three small mills that once stood here. There are at least three ghosts said to haunt the periphery of this quant New England village. I have learned of other phantoms in this immediate area, but their former identities are yet unknown. The first place one should visit on the way into Hopkins Mills is Tucker Hollow Road, an old carriage road with a reputation for ghosts.

Tucker Hollow Road runs along the border with the town of Scituate, between Route 101 and Route 6. This narrow dirt track is surrounded by thick woods and sparsely inhabited by only a few homes. The road can be a bit spooky to travel on late at night. There was a heartbreaking suicide and one ghastly

murder that both occurred on Tucker Hollow Road. The people
I spoke to about the road's history were unaware of any ghost
stories attributed to these two deaths. Even so, with the passage of time, these morbid episodes have become part of the
road's story and added to its mystique. The best-known tale of
Tucker Hollow Road is that of Aunt Lonnie Davis, an old recluse
who lived in a house set back from the road. Before she passed
away, the old woman told the folks of Hopkins Mills that no
one was to live in her house after she died. She had instructed
them to pull her home down and not to leave so much as two
boards nailed together or she would haunt the house. The house
remained standing for a time after Aunt Lonnie's death. The
story goes that anyone who ventured inside felt a cold breath
on the back of the neck. The men of the village eventually got
together and took the old house down. Legend has it that one
of the men deliberately left two boards behind that were still
nailed together. Today, this private parcel of land is still referred
to as "The Ghost Lot." Some people believe Aunt Lonnie's ghost
can sometimes be seen sitting on the stone wall of the Hopkins-Tucker Lot (Historical Cemetery #FR027) on Tucker Hollow Road. The Hopkins-Ide Lot (Historical Cemetery #FR026)
is located closer to Aunt Lonnie's old homestead, and if you ask
me, it's much creepier. It looks and feels like the perfect burial
ground for an old witch to haunt. However, two people from
Hopkins Mills have told me that there are stories about people seeing a very strange old woman sitting atop the stone wall
of the Hopkins-Tucker Lot. Those who were brave enough to
take a second look said the old woman was gone in an instant.
Why Aunt Lonnie haunts this serene and peaceful cemetery is
not understood. Perhaps she has a bone to pick with one of the
departed whose remains are buried in the lot.

   Take a right turn out of Tucker Hallow Road and head west
on Route 6. The long, steep hill you will find yourself driving
down is called Dolly Cole Hill. It is named after a woman who

A picture of the Ram Tail swimming hole taken in the ultraviolet-to-infrared light spectrum. The ghost of Betsey Grayson haunts this pool of water.

was well liked and a respected member of the community. She died in 1860 at the age of ninety-one and rests in peace along-side her husband, Hugh, and their son, Hugh Jr., in the Hopkins Mills Cemetery. The brook that flows under Old Danielson Pike and the low bridge there are both named for her. There is a popular misnomer that Dolly Cole is the white lady that haunts Hopkins Mills. Locals have always identified the ghost as that of a drowning victim who died six months after Dolly had passed away from natural causes.

On December 20, 1860, seventy-four-year-old Betsey Grayson drowned in the Ponagansett River while trying to fill her pail with water. The river's fast current must have pulled her off the embankment. Her body was found a few days later downstream in a swamp meadow. Shortly after Betsey Grayson's body was taken back to Scituate, Rhode Island, and buried in the family plot, her ghost began appearing along the riverbank and around the small group of mill houses where she once lived.

The ruins of the Ram Tail Factory photographed in the early 1900s. (Photo courtesy of Donna Mooney)

Her cottage is long gone, but fishermen have been reporting sightings of a strange woman on the banks of the Ponagansett in Hopkins Mills for decades. Betsey Grayson's ghost has also been seen by the bridge on Ram Tail Road. The road runs from the center of Hopkins Mills (off Old Danielson Pike) and crosses over Route 6. The Hopkins Mills Cemetery is on the left, and only a few hundred feet past the cemetery is the small bridge. There was a mill dam constructed on the Ponagansett River in the early 1800s that caused the river to back up and create a deep pool on the east side of the bridge. The locals called it the Ram Tail swimming pool, and this was the spot where the residents of Hopkins Mills would go swimming on hot summer days. There were some drowning accidents there. Apparently, the sediment at the bottom of the pool is an awful, thick muck. Some referred to it as "the sucking mud." Children were told they could only go swimming there if they went with a group and stayed away from the bottom of the pool. Diving into the water and hitting the bottom could get one stuck fast. My friend

Keith Johnson told me he jumped into the pool in the 1970s and nearly drowned when he too got stuck in the mud. The pool is still there, but it is not as wide and deep as it used to be.

I'm told it's a great spot to fish. A local fisherman told me about something strange that happened to him and a couple of his friends while they were fishing at the old Ram Tail swimming pool. The fisherman (name withheld) didn't know that the area was supposed to be haunted, and I hadn't mentioned anything to him about my interest in the paranormal. He said the incident took place one summer evening around eight o'clock. The setting sun was still providing enough light to cast their fishing lines one more time. The three of them were standing there quietly when the water at the center of the pool began to bubble and turn. Out of the rippling water came a milky white vapor that took on the vague form of a woman before it floated off into the woods. The fisherman told me that he and his friends grabbed their stuff and ran. He has never gone back, regardless of the great fishing.

Rhode Island's most famous haunted site is located only a few hundred yards down the Ponagansett from the old swimming pool. Walk into the woods along the dirt track and you will come to an old carriage trail that runs parallel to the Ponagansett River. What is left of the old dam is very easy to see. Look around long enough and the scant remains of the Foster Woolen Manufactory will also become clear. Better known as The Ram Tail Factory, this location was recorded in the 1885 Rhode Island State Census as being haunted. It might be the only census in the history of the United States that has a notation such as this.

In 1813 William Potter formed a business partnership with his son Olney, brother-in-law Jonathan Ellis, and his two sons-in-law, Marvin Round and Peleg Walker. Their goal was to build a fulling mill for the processing of raw wool and the manufacture of yarn and cloth. They purchased land less than a mile south of Hopkins Mills alongside the Ponagansett River and set up a mill and village the locals called the Ram Tail Factory. All went well until 1822 when Peleg Walker discovered he was living beyond his means and found himself in debt for $500. The once-successful Walker was then put into a humiliating position where he had to hand over his holdings in the factory to William and Olney Potter. Town records show the transition of property wasn't final until "May 19, 1822, at about one quarter of an hour before one o'clock AM." Since it had been Walker's responsibility to shut the mill down and secure the buildings every night, he wouldn't give up his duty or the keys until everything was official and he was no longer an equal partner. Peleg Walker is said to have argued with the Potters and told them that the next time they took the keys to the mill from him it would be from the pocket of a dead man. On the morning of May 19, 1822, the employees had to break a window to get into the locked mill. There they found Walker on the floor, with his throat cut and the keys to the mill in his pocket. Peleg Walker had apparently taken his life right on the date and time he had ceased to be a man of means.

The legend says that after Peleg Walker was buried in the Potter family's plot, strange things began to happen at the mill. The mill would supposedly start up in the middle of the night, and the factory bell would ring at midnight until the Potters took the rope down. These unsettling events are said to have made many of the employees leave. Whether because of hard economic times or the ghost of Peleg Walker, the mill closed down for good by 1850. One night in 1873, someone set the vacant mill building on fire. Some say it was vandalism; others say the building was burned to rid the Ram Tail of Peleg Walker's ghost.

If the fire was meant to cleanse the area of its ghost, it didn't work. People are still reporting seeing a strange light in the woods near the factory ruins that they believe is Peleg Walker's lantern light. The epitaph on Peleg's gravestone says it best: "Life, how short. Eternity, how long."

Connecticut

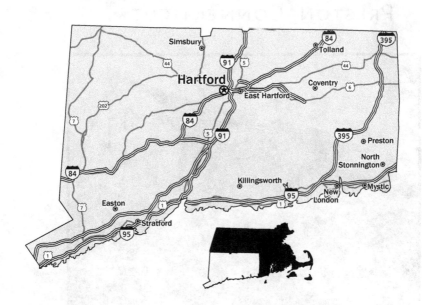

Coventry
Nathan Hale Homestead

East Hartford
Makens Bemont House Museum

Easton
The White Lady of Union
Cemetery

Hartford
Mark Twain House and Museum

Killingworth
Killingworth Café

Mystic
Whitehall Mansion Inn

New London
New London Ledge Lighthouse

North Stonington
The John York House

Preston
Captain Grant's, 1754

Simsbury
Abigail's Grille and Wine Bar

Stratford
Boothe Memorial Park and
Museum

Tolland
Benton Homestead Museum

CHAPTER 15

Captain Grant's, 1754
PRESTON, CONNECTICUT

CAPTAIN GRANT'S 1754 is an acclaimed bed-and-breakfast situated in the historic village of Poquetanuck (1687), in the town of Preston, Connecticut. As its name suggests, the house was built in 1754 by William Grant, a sea captain, who would set sail from nearby Poquetanuck Cove and often journeyed to Honduras with cargoes of grist (grain) to trade for fine mahogany. During one of these long trips, Grant suffered an illness aboard ship and died. He was thirty-two years old. The ship's crew brought the body of Captain Grant back home to be buried in the town's cemetery, which is located across the street from his former home. His widow, Mercy Adelaide Grant, continued to live in the house with their three children until she passed away in her late eighties. The property stayed within the family for three generations, and the house can be found listed on the National Register of Historic Places as the Grant home. I visited the cemetery and located the couple's graves. Although badly weatherworn and difficult to read, their gravestones are still standing. A strange fact about the plot is that one of William and Mercy's sons is interred right next to them in an unmarked grave. For some unknown reason his stone was taken sometime ago. It was later replaced, but that stone has also disappeared. Captain William Grant II and his wife are buried nearby with their markers intact. None of the neighboring graves show any signs of vandalism, so it is a mystery why this Grant's gravestone was singled out.

Sometime in the early twentieth century, the Grant house was purchased by the Taylor sisters. The building was then divided into two separate living spaces because the Taylor sisters hated each other. The story goes that the siblings never spoke to one another the entire time they lived there. When the sisters passed away, they too were buried in the cemetery across the street, side by side. Presumably, they're still not speaking to each other. The Congdon family was next to own the property. After their tenure in the home, the building sat unoccupied for a few years until it came up for sale in 1994. That's when Carol Matsumoto bought the neglected structure with the intention of bringing the old house back to life and opening it up as a bed-and-breakfast. No one said anything to her about the place being haunted. As far as Carol knew, the house never had a reputation for being haunted. However, as the renovations got underway, she could sense there was something unusual about the Grant home.

For two years, Carol and her husband, Ted, put a great deal of effort into rebuilding the house while keeping much of its original structure intact. They used authentic eighteenth-

The graves of Captain William Grant and his wife, Mercy

century building materials as well as pieces they knew had been removed from the building and stored away by past owners. When the work was completed in 1996, Captain Grant's 1754 opened for business. Once Carol and Ted had settled in, they started hearing the unmistakable sound of someone stomping around in the attic between the hours of four and five o'clock in the morning. This annoying racket does not manifest every morning, but often enough to be recognized by management and their staff as "the ghost in the attic." Apologies and explanations are served up along with breakfast to guests who have had their sleep disturbed by this rude phantom. About ten years ago, a New York City police detective and his wife were staying in the Adelaide Room, which is directly beneath the attic. He came downstairs in the morning, demanding that his money be refunded. When Carol asked him why, he answered back, "Because between four and five o'clock this morning, your husband was stomping around in the attic above us." Mrs. Matsumoto politely explained to the detective that there is a ghost in the attic who does this from time to time, and she would prove it to him after breakfast. When the detective was shown the attic, he saw for himself that it was absolutely impossible for anyone to have walked across the floor due to all the stacks of antique lumber being stored up there at the time. He no longer wanted his money back. In fact, he made reservations for Halloween.

Carol believes she may have identified the ghost in the attic by using a pair of divining rods sent to her as a gift by a woman who had stayed at the B&B. Most people think divining rods (or dowsing rods) are used by silly, superstitious folks to find hidden water sources and lost items. The truth is, divining rods do work if they are used properly. Ask anyone who works for a company that drills water wells. In ghosthunting, divining rods can be used to ask direct questions that have a "yes" or "no" answer. Carol brought the rods into the attic and asked the noisy ghost questions based on her knowledge of the property's history. Starting with the names of the last owners and working her way back into the past, she got a positive response when she asked, "Are you a male member of the Whipple family?" The Whipples were the original owners of the land, before Captain Grant's time. When she asked, "Is your age less than forty years?" Carol got another positive answer. The original cemetery for the town is located less than two hundred yards from the back of the house, and when she asked, "Are you buried in the cemetery behind the house?" the rods responded with another positive swing. What had inspired Carol to try this method of spirit communication was a divining session conducted by some guests who were holding a family reunion at the house in the summer of 2010. By going through the alphabet and asking questions with a "yes" or "no" answer, they got the name of a child, Deborah Adams. When the guest asked Deborah if she was buried across the street or out back, the rods responded with a positive swing to the cemetery out back. Mrs. Matsumoto had her groundskeeper, John, go out to the old cemetery and remove the overgrowth that was concealing the headstones from view. When the weeds and vines were cleared away, they discovered the graves of a young girl named Deborah Adams and a twenty-four-year-old male member of the Whipple family.

The ghost of Deborah Adams is suspected of being responsible for the moving and hiding of objects. One afternoon, two guests were relaxing downstairs in the front room by the door to the patio. In the room was a small table with a chess set on it. The pieces for the set were made from carved stone, which gave them considerable weight. The sound of something hitting the floor broke the silence in the room. It was a king chess piece. The guests looked at each other, not knowing what to say. One of them got up from his chair and put the piece back onto the board in its proper place. A moment later, the two of them were shocked to see the piece leap off the board and hit the floor with enough force to break the top off the king. The chess set is no longer on the table; it was removed due to lack of interest from those on this side of the veil.

Little Miss Adams may also be the culprit who has hidden a sand-filled doorstop that is made to look like a girl's doll. This cute doorstop has disappeared from the Adelaide room quite a few times, only to turn up in locations where it should not have been. The funniest disappearing act from the Adelaide Room involved a spray bottle filled with window cleaner. One busy morning, all the rooms at the B&B had been vacated at the same time and were scheduled to be filled right back up that very afternoon, so Carol and her staff had to get them cleaned up and ready for their next guests. Each member of the team had his specific chore in order to get the rooms prepared. Carol took the job of cleaning all the glass and metal surfaces. When one of the staff asked her to come and inspect another room, Carol set the bottle of cleaner down on a glass-topped table in the Adelaide Room as

This doll doorstop will sometimes go missing and then turn up later in an unexpected place somewhere the inn.

she stepped out the door. When she came back to the Adelaide Room, the cleaner was gone. They all looked for it in every room, upstairs and downstairs, but there was no spray bottle to be found anywhere. They gave up looking for it and finished the rooms in time for their next group of guests. Nearly a week later, one of the cleaning girls called out from upstairs for Ted and Carol to come to the Amy Room. As they entered the room, the girl pointed to the floor; there in the middle of the rug was the missing bottle of cleaner. They all had a good laugh over that one.

In addition to Mr. Whipple in the attic and Deborah, Carol believes there are other spirits in the house. A guest reported seeing the apparition of a woman wearing a full-length, blue dress with a white apron, standing at the top of the inside staircase. From the woman's description, Carol thinks it was the ghost of Mercy Adelaide Grant. Psychics have picked up on a young black girl who they say is looking for her mother. This could be accurate since the house is said to have been used by the Underground Railroad during the Civil War.

The most startling paranormal event at Captain Grant's also occurred in the Adelaide Room. One of the young women who worked for the Matsumotos was an atheist. Her name was Amy.

She did not believe in the existence of ghosts. Whenever a guest asked Amy about the building's haunted reputation she would always tell them, without hesitation, there are no such things as ghosts. During her normal daily routine she noticed that the metal blinds in the Adelaide Room, on three consecutive days, had a gap in the same spot, as if someone had pulled them apart with their fingers to look out the window. Each time Amy found them in this unsightly condition she straightened them out. The third time she had to fix the blinds, Amy's view on ghosts changed. Carol and the others were downstairs when they heard her scream. She was still screaming when they got upstairs to find out what was going on. Amy was so upset that no one could make any sense of what she was trying to say. Once they finally got her to relax enough to find out what had happened, she did her best to explain. Amy told them that she was standing in front of the window when a young girl appeared out of thin air and passed right through her outstretched arms as she was fixing the blinds. Amy had to take the next three days off to come to terms with what had happened. To her credit, she returned to work, and even though she said she would never, ever clean the Adelaide Room again, she did so that same day.

The building adjacent to Captain Grant's 1754 is the Avery Home, built in 1790. It, too, is on the National Register of Historic Places. The Matsumotos have the Holly and Margaret Rooms to offer in this beautiful eighteenth-century home. A photograph taken in the house by Carol before renovations began suggests that this building is also haunted. The picture shows a vaguely human-shaped mist in a doorway. After the renovations were completed, the same anomaly was captured in front of the Christmas tree. Carol has postcards available with this ghostly image on the front. Who is this spirit? Bring your divining rods and stay for a weekend, you just might find out for yourself.

North Stonington, Connecticut

North Stonington is a peaceful and attractive rural area in southeastern Connecticut. At the intersection of Pendleton Hill Road and Clarks Fall Road, one will find the historic John York House. It was built in 1741 as a private home, but by the time of the Revolutionary War, its owner, John York, opened a small tavern in the house to profit from the increased traffic on the Providence-to-New London post road. Two of his patrons are said to be responsible for the first haunting to start there.

The legend claims that two soldiers got into an argument over a woman while drinking in the tavern. A physical altercation then ensued and one stabbed the other before running off. The stabbed soldier died in a pool of blood on the floor of the tavern and his former friend hung himself at another, undocumented location. It is said that the murdered soldier's spirit continues to inhabit the house. The floorboards that were discolored by his blood were turned over to hide the stain.

There is a second death that is believed to have occurred inside the house. That incident is said to have happened on the steep staircase that leads from the kitchen area to an upstairs bedroom. A man who had had too much to drink supposedly fell down the stairs and broke his neck. He too is thought to haunt the house.

In 1964 Hugo and Miriam Wilms bought the property and moved in with their three sons. They were unaware of the house's morbid history or its ghost stories. The first strange thing that the family noticed was that a barometer in the entryway kept coming off the wall. Hugo Wilms would remount it, each time using longer screws. Until one day the barometer flew off the wall and smashed into little pieces.

The paranormal activity increased with time. The family

sometimes heard footsteps on the back stairs leading up to the attic. What made the footsteps even more extraordinary was the fact that there was a locked door to go through before one could reach the attic. The boys' beds would sometimes move in the middle of the night. The oldest son once felt a hand press down hard on his shoulder while he was lying in bed. The pressure held him to the mattress and paralyzed him with fear so badly that he almost couldn't breath. When the unseen hand finally released him, he turned on the light and examined his shoulder. He could see marks on his skin where the hand had pinned him.

In 2010 Ray Bendici interviewed Dan Wilms (the Wilms's youngest son) for the Web site "Damned Connecticut" and asked him about the years his family lived in the John York House. Wilms said his family wasn't really frightened by the ghosts; instead, they tried to understand them. A photographer for a local newspaper suggested to the Wilms family that they should bring in Ed and Lorraine Warren, Connecticut's famous paranormal investigators. The Warrens brought a psychic with them who picked up on the soldiers who had fought in the tavern. The psychic felt the murdered soldier was earthbound and haunting the house.

Dan Wilms said there is a woman haunting the house as well. Several people saw her ghost during the time the Wilmses lived there. On one occasion, a man who had come to their home to pick up some old bed frames saw the female phantom standing in the hallway on the second floor. Dan Wilms saw her once more, right before his family moved out in 1987.

Ten years after the Wilms family left, David and Leea Grote bought the house and turned it into a bed-and-breakfast. The Grotes said that they hadn't experienced anything "too unusual," but some of their guests had reported hearing and seeing odd things during their stays. The house was resold in 2007 to a couple from Rhode Island and at present is unoccupied.

CHAPTER 16

Nathan Hale Homestead
COVENTRY, CONNECTICUT

Museum staff and visitors have experienced many strange moments at the Nathan Hale Homestead.

"I ONLY REGRET THAT I HAVE but one life to lose for my country." So said twenty-one-year-old Nathan Hale on September 22, 1776. He made this patriotic statement in New York City on the occasion of his own execution. His crime: espionage in a time of war. Nathan was one of eight sons born in Coventry, Connecticut, to Richard and Elizabeth Hale. He started courses at Yale University when he was fourteen years old and graduated with top honors four years later. The young Mr. Hale became a teacher and held special classes for girls, feeling strongly that education was just as important for girls as it was for boys. He began making fiery speeches for independence soon after news of the conflict at Lexington and Concord, Massachusetts, reached his corner of New England. Already a lieutenant in his local militia at this time, he would become a captain in the Continental Army in March of 1776.

After the British Royal Army and Navy were forced to retreat from Boston, they headed straight for New York City and its deep harbor. The city fell into British hands after their swift victory on Long Island. It then became vital for General Washington and his officers to get intelligence on the King's forces in and around the now-occupied city. Captain Hale volunteered to be inserted behind enemy lines to gather any and all relevant information, despite being warned that anyone caught in the act of spying would be hanged by the neck. On September 21, 1776, nine days after he arrived, a horrible fire swept through lower Manhattan. Historians are still debating about who or what started this great blaze. The British were certain it was the act of American terrorists. They rounded up some two hundred men as suspects. Nathan Hale was one of them. While being questioned about his identity and purpose in the city, damaging evidence was found on his person. Nathan bravely admitted to who and what he really was. In doing so, he sealed his own fate.

Just like the actual cause of the fire, historians are not settled on Hale's exact last words. A British Officer named John Montresor, who was present at Hale's execution, would later tell Captain William Hull, while under a flag of truce, Nathan stood strong and did speak the now-famous quote. Word of Nathan Hale's bravery spread through the colonies, touching the hearts of many, encouraging them to join in the fight for freedom and independence in any way they could.

Nathan's death wasn't the only harsh sacrifice made by the Hale family for our country. Five of his brothers also served in the military. Sometime after the war's end, three of them would die from wounds they received in battle. Their widows and children came to live at the Hale estate, participating in all the hard work that did lead to a level of prosperity for Richard Hale. By this time, the home that young Nathan left behind no longer existed. It had been replaced by a fine, two-story, Georgian-style house. Mr. Hale became an important and well-respected figure in the community. One local service he performed was Justice of the Peace. Legal disputes between neighbors would be heard out and weighed by Richard at the Hale homestead. Court sessions were held in a downstairs room referred to, appropriately enough, as the Justice Room.

In the 1820s members of the Hale family sold the property. The house and its lands would not thrive and prosper as they had in Richard and Elizabeth's time. By the turn of the twentieth century, around 1914, a wealthy and somewhat eccentric attorney from New Haven named George Dudley Seymour bought the homestead with the goal of bringing it back to it original condition. The house was in a bad state, but that did not keep Mr. Seymour from his dream, for he had been a great admirer of Nathan Hale ever since he was a little boy.

A man with a mission, George kept at it, saving whatever he could and replacing what needed to be replaced, all the while paying attention to historical accuracy. He discovered through research a written account of Nathan Hale's profile having been drawn on a door in the house. It was a common technique in the eighteenth century to use a candle to cast a shadow of a person's profile onto a surface and then trace it as a keepsake. Seymour found the door and uncovered the hand-drawn silhouette. Visitors can view this remarkable artifact on display in the museum.

The first ghost story told about the Hale Homestead comes from around 1920. George Dudley Seymour was very proud of what he had accomplished with the old property and would often bring friends and colleagues to the house for weekend stays. On one of these visits, a guest, so excited to be arriving at the historic home of a great American patriot like Hale, ran up to a front window to take a look inside. What he saw through the windowpane gave him quite a shock. Standing inside the room was a figure dressed in Colonial attire; the figure then disappeared. It is not known whether the guest stayed the weekend or not.

When Mr. Seymour died in 1945, he left the property to Connecticut Landmarks. The majority of the land is now preserved as the Nathan Hale State Forest, a beautiful wooded area in which to hike and enjoy nature. The farm is still active. Every Sunday, from June 6 to October 31, the Coventry Regional Farmers market is held with a large public turnout. The house, barn, and stone walls stand much as they did in Hale's time. Even the paint scheme is accurate to the period, thanks to painstaking research. The home is decorated with authentic furnishings, and every little knickknack is correct in its detail. There are also items original to the house, one being Nathan Hale's own fowling piece. With all the care and attention given to the preservation of this place in which so much heartfelt energy has been spent, it is no wonder the staff and some visitors have had encounters with those from its past.

The museum's director, Bev York, is not a believer in the paranormal, but she is proud to be part of the Hale Homestead. I first met Ms. York with some of the museum's guides two years earlier, and I found them all to be quite well informed about the Hales, their home, and history in general. Sitting at a table in the home's kitchen, Bev talks about the docents that work at the homestead and what they think about the notion that the house may be haunted. "Some know the stories, because they're good old stories and the visitors want to know," she says. "Some believe and some don't. Some won't be here alone. They don't like to lock up alone."

The stories of ghostly encounters I was told on my first visit to the museum have remained vivid in my mind. Ms. York knows these accounts well and helped to make sure I had the facts straight for this book. Here are some of the tales from the volunteers and staff.

A cleaning lady who comes in on a regular basis has had a few remarkable moments. On several occasions, after making and fluffing up a bed in one of the upstairs rooms, she has found an unsettling impression in the mattress, as if someone has lain down on the bed. Keep in mind that she works alone, and the house was always locked when this event happened. One day she was downstairs in the kitchen when she clearly heard a conversation in the next room (a small, modern kitchen for the business offices) between two persons. She was sure they were talking about the small garden in the backyard. As she opened the door to the office kitchen, the voices suddenly stopped and she found no one there. The sounds of footsteps have also been heard coming down the stairs from a small attic above the kitchen. They are believed to be the ghost of a young girl who may have worked as a servant or kitchen aide.

During visitors' hours, there are always two guides at the homestead. They take turns on duty. One will watch the barn and gift shop, while the other conducts a tour of the grounds. As one of the docents entered the house with a small group one afternoon, they all noticed someone walking around on the second floor. Finding it strange that the other volunteer was in the house instead of the barn, the guide called upstairs. A male voice answered back, "I'll be down in a moment." As the tour continued on it became obvious that the footsteps had stopped, and no one had come down the staircase. Nobody was found to be upstairs, and the other volunteer had been out in the barn the whole time. As Bev York said, some of the staff don't like to close up alone at night. One evening a staff member heard loud sobbing coming from the upstairs as she was setting the alarm and locking the door. She felt no desire to investigate the unnerving sound. She just locked up and left the poor soul to itself. On another night at closing time, a volunteer named Elizabeth and her skeptical husband were standing outside when they both saw a strange light in the attic window. Not only did this light have an unnatural look about it, the only light bulb up there (had it been on) would have been blocked from view by the chimney stack. They checked the attic; the light was off and no explanation was found for the odd glow.

The most amusing moment involved the ghost of Richard Hale. A volunteer named Leslie was taking a man and his young son on a tour of the house. While it is a house, it is also a museum filled with objects that need to be treated with respect and care. The visitor understood that, but his rambunctious and bored little boy fussed and ran about the house, embarrassing the man to no end. No matter how hard he tried, he could not control the child. At one point the boy ran off from his father and went right into the Justice Room. After a moment of silence, he ran right back to his father and Leslie, upset about the man who was looking at him in the room. Leslie took the boy by the hand to show him the man was just a portrait of Mr. Hale. The little boy insisted the man in the painting was standing on the other side of the room and was looking right at him. The little animal was now tamed and wanted his father to please take him home. It seems that Justice of the Peace Hale once again restored law and order in his home.

Spotlight On: Benton Homestead Museum
Tolland, Connecticut

At 160 Metcalf Road in Tolland, Connecticut, stands the Daniel Benton homestead, the town's oldest surviving house. The original portion of the structure dates back to 1720. As the family grew, the house developed into a full Cape Cod style with an ell at the rear. The Benton's lived there and farmed the land for six generations. In 1932 Florrie Bishop Bowering, a dietician and radio personality, purchased the property. Bowering called this place home until her death in 1968. The following owners, Charles B. Goodstein and William A. Shocket, decided to donate the former Benton home to the Tolland Historical Society, which then opened the house as a public museum in 1969.

Florrie Bishop Bowering left many of the home's subtle architectural treasures alone, but she did make some changes to the structure in order to make it a little more comfortable and

Spotlight On:
Benton Homestead Museum
(continued)

convenient for twentieth-century living. However, her respectful alterations to the old Benton home may have caused a stir in the building's psychic makeup, because it was during her time in the house that the stories about ghosts roaming the property came to light.

Bowering retained a live-in maid who claimed that she would frequently see the apparition of a young woman in a wedding dress moving through the house. The maid also said she would hear the sound of a woman sobbing so often that she became accustomed to it. The phantom bride is believed to be the ghost of Jemima Barrows, a young, brokenhearted woman who died in the house and was buried on the property. Jemima Barrow's story is a sad tale. She had fallen in love with Elisha Benton, one of Daniel Benton's grandsons.

A sample of the Hessian's graffiti left on a beam in the cellar. This photograph was taken in the ultraviolet-to-infrared light spectrum to pick out hidden detail in the old writing.

Elisha wanted Jemima to be his wife, but the Benton family felt she was beneath their station and forbade any union between them. The couple would not give up their feelings for one another and held hope that one day they would be together. In 1776 Elisha Benton and two of his brothers answered the Lexington alarm and marched off to war. It is said that Elisha promised Jemima that he would return home and asked her to wait for him.

The three Benton brothers were captured by the British and made prisoners of war. Elisha's two brothers died in captivity, but he was later released in a prisoner exchange. During Elisha Benton's imprisonment on a ship in New York harbor, he contracted the dreaded disease small pox. By the time the British set him free, he was a condemned man. Elisha made it home, but when he arrived, his loved ones had to stay clear of him for fear of contracting the illness themselves.

It is believed that his mother was the only person who was allowed to stay with him in the home after it was closed off and quarantined. She would have developed a natural immunity to small pox due to her constant contact with the family's dairy cows. Regardless of the danger and the quarantine, Jemima Barrows came to the Benton home and insisted on helping with Elisha's care. Elisha Benton died a few weeks later on January 21, 1777. His body was wrapped in a shroud and removed from the house through a ground floor window. Elisha Benton was laid to rest at the base of the wall by the home's carriageway. On February 28, 1777, Jemima Barrows herself died in quarantine at the Benton home and was buried on the other side of the carriageway. The strict quarantine dictated that Elisha's and Jemima's bodies could not leave the property; they had to be buried quickly to prevent the threat of the disease spreading. Because the two were not married, it was considered improper for them to be buried next to one another. This eternal separation from the man she loved enough to die for is thought to be the reason why Jemima Barrows's weeping spirit haunts the Benton homestead.

Spotlight On:
Benton Homestead Museum
(continued)

Another ghost that has been spotted here is a Colonial-era soldier. He has been seen at the front door of the house, standing there as if he is waiting to be let inside. Witnesses are not clear about whether the ghost is dressed in an American uniform (which would suggest it is the spirit of Elisha Benton) or possibly the uniform of a German Hessian mercenary. Twenty-one German prisoners of war were detained at the Benton homestead and billeted in the home's stone cellar. They lived there for eighteen months and worked for the Bentons and their neighbors. One can still make out words written by these men on a beam in the cellar. Three of the Hessians remained in the town of Tolland, and their descendents are still part of the community. For sometime now, people have reported hearing voices coming from the old stone cellar, speaking in a language that they couldn't quite make out. No one has been able to decipher what the prisoners wrote on the beam either, since it is believed to be an old and forgotten German dialect.

When I visited the Benton homestead, the museum's director, Gail White Usher, told me that she has never experienced anything unusual in the house—nothing that she couldn't explain rationally. The director did share with me something she was told in 2007, when workman were on the property conducting major repair work to the nearly three-hundred-year-old home. Apparently some of the men said they heard footsteps, voices, and even caught glimpses of movement past doorways and windows. Apparently, they were a little shaken by the activity, especially when they couldn't find anyone else in the house with them.

CHAPTER 17

Boothe Memorial Park and Museum

STRATFORD, CONNECTICUT

The Boothe Family home. This picture shows the door from which the Spiritualist group fled and the second-floor window where the man in black was seen waving his lantern.

DAVID AND STEPHEN BOOTHE transformed a hay barn on their farm into a clock tower building in 1913 as a way to celebrate the Boothe family's 250th anniversary in the Putney section of Stratford, Connecticut. The clock tower they added to the top of the barn came from an abandoned church in Massachusetts. They didn't pay cash for the tower and its handmade, cherry wood clock; they traded a carpet sweeper for it. Once the

The Anniversary Clock Tower. The mysterious man in black has also been seen walking around the clock tower with his lantern in hand.

construction was completed, David and Stephen dubbed their new building the Anniversary Clock Tower and opened it to the public as a museum containing items from their family's past and early American history.

As the years went on, the Boothe brothers continued to expand their museum and added more structures to the property, most of which were designed and built by David Boothe. One of David's more interesting projects is the "Technocratic Cathedral." Made from large, squared timbers, this log cabin-like structure has no vertical lines in its form, only horizontal. He did not use any nails in its construction; the huge lengths of redwood that make up this unique building are held in place by galvanized dowels. The windows are thick blocks of glass, stacked together and held in place by the tight fit of the timbers. The cathedral was originally designed to be taller, but David changed the plans when he found out how much the town was going to tax him if he went any further with the building.

When the two brothers passed away in 1949, they left the land and its buildings to the town, with the stipulation that the property would continue as a park and museum. Regrettably, the town was unable to maintain the property. The buildings, including the Boothes' home, fell into disrepair. Two men were hired as caretakers to keep an eye on the twenty-four buildings and the Boothes extensive collection of historic items, but there were problems with the way the caretakers performed their duties. During their time on the property, many important pieces went missing from the museum.

The Boothe Park Commission was appointed in 1982 to assess the property and determine what work was needed to save the buildings, which were all in very poor condition. The first person to chair the commission was Bessie Burton, who held the position for nearly eight years. When I met with Ms. Burton at the Boothes' homestead, she told me that as the members of the commission began cataloging everything on the property, many interesting items belonging to the Boothe family were discovered. It was then agreed that all the buildings on the property should be restored in order to expand the museum and its exhibits. In 1984 a group called The Friends of Boothe Park was formed with the objective of bringing the park and museum back to life.

We sat in an office on the second floor of the Boothe house, and Bessie Burton began the conversation by informing me that, "I am not at all psychic, I don't have ESP, but some of the people I work with could feel cold drafts moving through the house and sometimes heard noises." She said that when the Boothe Park Commission first set up in the main house it seemed "very cold and unwelcoming." As the house came together and was put right, it became warmer and much more inviting, almost like it appreciated what the volunteers were doing.

Before the Friends of Boothe Park was formed, the house was used as a place for local clubs to meet and discuss their interests. One of the organizations that used the Boothe house for their meetings was a Rosicrucian group. Rosicrucianism is a belief system that delves into ancient mystical and philosophical doctrines. One night, the group assembled on the first floor in a circle with lighted candles and began calling out to some ancient force to hear them. Apparently, they got more than they expected. Every member of the group was suddenly overcome by a horrible wave of sickness that forced them outside onto the lawn where they all began to throw up. As one of the Rosicrucians began to recover from her nausea, she turned and looked back at the house. The woman claimed she saw a man wearing dark clothes and a tall black hat, standing at a window on the second floor. The male figure was also waving a glowing lantern in a manner that strongly suggested to the woman that he wanted the group to go away.

Over the years, people have reported seeing a man matching the same description walking the balcony of the clock tower. He is always dressed in dark clothes, wearing a stovepipe hat, and carrying a lantern. It is believed that he is the ghost of old man Boothe, David and Stephen's father, who died in 1909. Mr. Boothe was a devout Congregationalist and held a private pew at his church. The door to his pew is on display in the museum. Perhaps Mr. Boothe didn't care for what the Rosicrucian assembly was up to that night and wanted them out of his home. The clock tower is also a good vantage point for one to keep an eye on the homestead.

When the Friends of Boothe Park first opened the main house as part of the museum, only the first floor was accessible to the public. While conducting tours downstairs the guides would sometimes hear a woman's voice calling out from a room on the second floor, which was always kept locked. Whenever a staff member would go to investigate, the voice would trial off as they approached the door to the room. When they unlocked the door and searched the room, no one was ever found inside. The second floor was opened for museum space in 1985, and since then people have reported catching a glimpse of a woman in a black dress with a white apron at the top of the stairs near the very same room. This female ghost is most likely Mrs. Betsy Amelia Nichols Beardsley Boothe. The reason Mrs. Boothe's ghost is seen dressed in black might be because she is still in mourning for her first husband who died in battle during the American Civil War. She also lost her infant daughter to an illness and both of her parents all within a very short period of time. It seems the twenty-six-year-old Betsy married Mr. Boothe, who was twenty-four years her senior, out of sheer necessity.

Another room on the second floor has caused many people to become quite sad and upset soon after they enter it. The museum used to refer to the room as The Civil War Room because of the collection of Civil War-related items that were once displayed in there. On the very first day that the second floor was opened to the public, an elderly woman was being shown the Civil War Room when, as Bessie Burton said, "All of a sudden she burst into tears; she was just distraught. So her friend took her out of the room, and as soon as she got outside of the room, she was fine. But when she started to go back inside the room again she broke down with this overwhelming feeling of grief and sadness. We didn't think anything at the time, but it became a trend, and we've had over a hundred experiences like that with other people."

One stiflingly hot day, a couple from Alabama was in the Civil War Room with their four-year-old daughter. The little girl inexplicably developed goose bumps and began to shiver. As soon as they got her out of the room, she was fine. On another occasion, a group of film students from Fairfield University

The Nursery Room, formerly known as the Civil War Room, has caused some visitors to become very depressed when they stand in the small space.

were at Boothe Park to put together a video presentation for the museum. Every time they tried to shoot in the Civil War Room, their camera equipment would not function properly. The students could find no explanation for the failure. The museum has since removed the Civil War-related items from the room and put them on display in the clock tower building. The little room is currently set up as a nursery.

Transferring the Civil War exhibit out of the house didn't stop the strange behavior in the upstairs room. Visitors to the museum and the guides still have awkward moments in the Nursery Room, as it is now called. They have experienced cold spots and felt pressure on the backs of their necks as if a hand was grabbing them. Others have reported hearing a swishing sound, as if some unseen person had moved past them. The museum's staff has concluded that the war memorabilia could not have been influencing sensitive people to feel uneasy or break down emotionally; it is something about the room itself.

Bessie Burton was in the house when a most unnerving sound erupted from the Nursery Room. A local paranormal group had been allowed to conduct a ghost tour of Boothe Park and the museum, and while inside the main house, the tour was split into two groups taking turns on each floor. Ms. Burton was downstairs with one group while the other group was upstairs learning all about the strange happenings that have occurred in the Nursery Room. "We heard this incredibly loud noise crack through the building," said Bessie. Her first thought was, "what could have fallen," but nothing had fallen. Everyone present in the house agreed that the sound came from the second floor, and it had emanated from the Nursery Room.

Probably the eeriest incident to take place in the main house involved an encounter with a doppelganger. A doppelganger is a spirit that can take on the likeness of a living person who is present in the haunted environment. Two teenage girls who were working as docents one summer saw what they thought was their friend and co-worker, a girl named Jessica, walk past them and into a pantry located off of the dining room on the first floor. When this spitting image walked past them, they asked her to please grab them a couple of sodas out of the pantry. Within a few seconds, the real Jessica came towards them from another direction. The two teenagers could not understand how their friend could have come from that direction, and Jessica had no idea what they were talking about. When they checked the pantry it was empty, and no one could have walked away from it without being seen.

Spotlight On: The White Lady
of Union Cemetery
Easton, Connecticut

One of Connecticut's best-known ghosts haunts the Union Cemetery in Easton. The cemetery sits beside the centuries-old Easton Baptist Church near the intersection of Routes 59 and 136. The locals call the ghost "The White Lady," and she has been seen by dozens of witnesses since the mid-twentieth century.

The legend of The White Lady contains several explanations about who she was and how she came to haunt the cemetery and nearby Route 59. One account says she was buried in the cemetery after she died during childbirth, and her confused spirit is desperately looking for her child. Two other versions say she was the victim of foul play. She was either murdered near the turn of the twentieth century, her body thrown down a sinkhole behind the church; or her husband killed her sometime in the 1940s.

The Union Cemetery on Route 59 in Easton

Though her ghost has been seen moving about the cemetery late at night, most encounters take place on Route 59. The White Lady has a habit of appearing directly in front of people's cars as they drive by the Union Cemetery, causing them to break hard and swerve to avoid impact. Any driver who has stopped to make sure the woman is all right finds no one around. A local fireman driving by the cemetery one night thought he struck a dark-haired woman in a white dress, who had walked right out into the road. Not only did this man feel the impact, he also discovered a dent on the hood of his vehicle. A search of the area turned up nothing.

Writer and paranormal enthusiast Jeff Belanger told me he grew up in this part of Connecticut and had heard many people talk about the White Lady. Jeff was once shown a video clip that was shot by the legendary paranormal investigators Ed and Lorraine Warren, who staked out the Union Cemetery one night in 1990. The Warrens had set up a video camera on a tripod in front of the main gates to the old burial ground and waited to see if The White Lady would make an appearance. Later that night they recorded nearly six seconds of video that Jeff Belanger called "compelling."

Ed Warren told Belanger that at about 2:40 a.m., he heard the sound of a woman weeping in the cemetery. When Warren looked out into the field of headstones, he could see little points of light coalescing into the shape of a woman. This female form then began to move in his direction. Being the fearless ghosthunter that he was (Ed passed away in 2006), Ed tried to walk towards the specter, but as he did so, it dissipated and vanished from sight. Belanger said the video recording captured what looked like "a misty white form" taking shape into the outline of a human. The form then moved several feet through the graveyard before it faded into the ground by the front gates.

The Union Cemetery is closed after sunset, and the police do take notice of trespassers. So, if you do go for a visit, please be respectful.

CHAPTER 18

Abigail's Grille and Wine Bar
SIMSBURY, CONNECTICUT

The former Pettibone Tavern has been renamed Abigail's Grille and
Wine Bar, in honor of the female ghost that haunts the building.

RESEARCHING A HAUNTED LOCATION usually
reveals that popular legends explaining the ghostly activity are
more folklore than fact. But, fellow haunted road trippers, this
does not mean that the location isn't haunted; it only means too
many people have had fun telling campfire stories instead of
keeping their facts straight.

A ghost that has been seen or experienced at a specific location will often be identified as a person believed to have had a
connection to the haunted site. It is only logical to assume the

ghostly figure of a lady seen dressed in period costume is the same woman who is known to have lived on the property in question. Assumptions are poor substitutes for detailed research, however. It is possible the ghost may be that of a lesser-known person who once played a brief part in the property's history and has been forgotten through the passage of time.

Abigail's Grille and Wine Bar occupies an old building in Simsbury, Connecticut, with a ghost story attached to it that appears to be a perfect example of a good story superseding the facts. The popular legend of how the place became haunted is short and simple. The tale claims the husband of Abigail Pettibone came home sooner than expected from a whaling trip and caught her in bed with another man. Enraged by his wife's infidelity, the sailor killed Abigail and her lover with an ax, and Abigail Pettibone has haunted the building ever since. When I first started looking into this legend, some folks in Simsbury told me it was only a story created for publicity by one of the building's former owners in the 1970s. My own research left me with some doubt about the ax-murder story, but the witnesses I interviewed at Abigail's are certain that someone haunts the old tavern.

Jonathan Pettibone, Jr. was born in Simsbury on August 12, 1741. He was an educated man who took a deep interest in the town. His father was a farmer and also a colonel with the Eighteenth Connecticut Regiment of Militia. Jonathan served under his father in the War for Independence as a second lieutenant. He later rose to first lieutenant and then received the rank of colonel after the war. Pettibone, Sr. died in 1776 at Rye, New York, fighting against the British. Neither of these two men, or Jonathan Pettibone III, were ever sailors in the whaling trade.

Jonathan Pettibone, Jr. built a stagecoach tavern at this location around 1780. Indians burned the tavern to the ground about twenty years later, and Pettibone then rebuilt it on the original foundation.

In my research I could find no female member of the Pettibone family with the first name Abigail. Jonathan Pettibone, Jr.'s mother was named Martha (Humphrey); his wife's name was Hannah (Owen); and his son, Jonathan III, married a local woman named Fanny (Phelps). None of these unions produced a female child with the name Abigail. The only Abigail Pettibone I could find was originally from Canton, Connecticut, and she married David Phelps (the great-grandfather of Fanny Phelps) in 1731. Their sons, Elisha and Noah, helped Ethan Allen and his Green Mountain Boys capture Fort Ticonderoga in 1775. Abigail Phelps died in 1787 at the age of eighty-one. The Pettibone and Phelps families appear to have been people of exceptional character and well respected by the community of Simsbury.

When the era of stagecoach travel ended, the old tavern became a private residence. In the 1970s the Chart House chain of restaurants purchased the property. During their time in the building the ghost stories became known. It is also the time period when the tale of Abigail Pettibone came into being. Skeptics point to the absence of facts in Abigail's story as unarguable proof that the reports of paranormal activity in the building were nothing more than a publicity stunt used to generate business for the Chart House Restaurant. From what I have heard, the food and service during the Chart House years was very good, and there was no need for ghost stories to attract more customers. Restaurant managers are far too busy to do historic research and conduct ghosthunts, so it is likely someone simply concocted a good campfire story to tell customers who inquired about the building's ghostly activity.

The business did eventually change ownership and continued on as The Pettibone Tavern. The paranormal activity continued as well. Staff and management reported many startling events, most taking place early in the morning or after hours when the restaurant was closing for the night. Drinking glasses were frequently seen moving by themselves. One waitress is said

The ghost of a woman in white has been seen on these stairs.

to have found all the water glasses in the dining room standing straight up only moments after she had set them on the tables upside down.

Another strange story from the former Pettibone Tavern claims that a Hitchcock chair was found one morning in the middle of the dining room smashed to pieces. The manager discovered this weird act of vandalism when he opened the restaurant for business that day. The solid oak chair was perfectly fine when the manager had locked up the night before, and there were no signs of a break-in. Why anyone, living or dead, would want to destroy such a fine chair is hard to understand.

In January, 2008, a small fire broke out on the second floor in the middle of the night. The building's sprinkler system quickly extinguished the fire, but the firefighting system's alarm did not activate, resulting in extensive water damage caused by the sprinklers running for several hours. Not long after this ugly mishap, the property changed hands. The new owners took nearly a year to make substantial renovations to the building's interior and reopened as Abigail's Grille and Wine Bar.

I had the opportunity to sit with the general manager of Abigail's, Markus Lehofer, and ask him what he thought about the building's haunted reputation. Markus told me that he and his employer were not at all interested in the ghost stories when they first started up the new restaurant; they both felt the tales were an invention used by previous owners to attract customers. Markus said he became a little more open-minded, however, as some of his customers, who were either patrons or employees of the past two restaurants, began volunteering their own personal stories about the building and its ethereal inhabitants. Guests have openly talked to Markus and his staff about past occurrences such as furniture and tableware moving on their own, unexplainable drafts of icy cold air, and voices heard when no one else was around. One person talked about a particular night after closing time when he clearly heard the noise of a crowded tavern, complete with singing and the clanking of mugs. Another witness claimed he once saw the ghost of a little boy run through the upstairs bar and into the ladies' room. When the room was checked, no one was inside. These stories became even more believable for the crew at Abigail's when they too started seeing and hearing the same strange things.

Markus Lehofer said his one strange episode at Abigail's took place around 12:30 at night. He was talking with the bartender in the new bar room, which is located on the first floor by the front entrance, when a loud bang startled them. Markus said, "We knew it came from the lobby because the door (between the lobby and the bar) was open. I was like, 'What the heck was that!' So we went to check the lobby to see what fell." Markus and the bartender thought a glass bowl full of mints had fallen off the reception desk. It took them only a few short strides to reach the lobby from the bar. They noticed nothing broken or out of place.

Markus quickly checked both the men's and ladies' rooms and found everything in order. While he was in the ladies' room, the bartender called out to him, "Oh my God! Can you hear this, can you hear this?" Markus could only hear the sound of the exhaust fan in the restroom. When he stepped back into the lobby, the bartender looked right at him and said, "It sounded like someone was dragging furniture across the floor upstairs." The two of them went to the second floor, and, after looking all around, they couldn't find anything moved.

During my visit to Abigail's, I met two staff members, Kristin Ennaco and Jose Flores. Kristin told me she has had some unsettling moments in the tavern room on the second floor, all of them late at night. She has heard a woman call her by name several times, and the voice always sounds as if the woman is standing directly behind her. Kristin has been alone every time this has happened. I asked her if she had ever seen anything in the tavern upstairs, and she said, "I have seen glasses fly—not just fall over, but fly and smash." Kristin then added that she has also caught sight of someone walking around in the kitchen at times when the kitchen was closed.

Jose Flores has been working at Abigail's for two years and has also seen a figure moving around the kitchen area. Jose comes in very early in the morning to do cleaning and has felt a presence in that part of the building. Besides the occasional glimpse of a figure, Jose has also heard soft footsteps, like that of a woman, when he is the only person in the building. Two members of the kitchen staff told Jose that they have seen a woman dressed in white walking around the kitchen more than once. The restaurant's current owner reported seeing a ghostly hand floating in the hallway that leads to the offices behind the kitchen area. Perhaps it was the ghost, known as Abigail, waving hello to the tavern's new owner.

Spotlight On: Makens Bemont House Museum
East Hartford, Connecticut

The Bemont House in East Hartford was built in 1761 by Edmund Bemont. Four years later, he sold the house to his hardworking son, Makens. Makens Bemont was a successful saddle maker who later increased his fortune by buying and selling property in East Hartford. Members of the Bemont family lived in the home well into the nineteenth century. The house is more commonly referred to as "The Huguenot House," but no one is really sure where this name came from. The Huguenots were a sect of French Protestants from the sixteenth and seventieth centuries, many of whom came to North America to escape religious persecution. Since there is little recorded information on the history of the house, it maybe safe to assume that a French Protestant family lived in the home after the Bemont family's time there. The last private owner of the house was a man named Adolph Rosenthal, who donated the property to the East Hartford Historical Society in 1968. Two years later the society sold the land and moved the two-story house from the corner of Tolland Street and Burnside Avenue to Martin Park (307 Burnside Avenue), where it now stands along with two other historic structures, the Goodwin Schoolhouse and the Burnham Blacksmith Shop. As far as anyone knows, in the 190 years that the house stood at its original location, there were never any accounts of ghostly phenomena associated with the place.

Before the Bemont House was moved, it was in need of extensive renovations and repair work. After it was brought to Martin Park in 1971, volunteers went to work while members of the community raised money to hire professionals to handle the major restorations. Not long after the building contractors were brought in, they reported hearing hammering in the house from rooms where no one was working. One worker claimed that when he arrived at the house early one morning, he could hear the sound of someone working inside the house. When he tried to open the door, he found it still locked. The hammering then stopped and a short time later, when the rest of the crew showed up at the park, it was clear that no one had been in the house.

Members of the historical society gave this poltergeist the nickname "Benny," short for Benjamin, meaning "son of the right hand." The ghost is also believed to be responsible for tools disappearing, freak injuries to the builders, and strange construction mishaps. His hammering is still heard in the house on occasions. Don Carter of the New England Paranormal Video Research Group (NEPVRG) feels that the ghost is actually named Henry. The psychic who works with NEPVRG picked up on the name Henry while the group was conducting an investigation of the house in 2006. Their psychic didn't feel that Henry had ever lived in the home, but felt he was "deeply invested" in it. Don Carter learned through research that a retiree named Henry had volunteered his time and skills in the early days of the home's renovations. A local newspaper mentioned this man in an article about the repairs being done to the old home. He told the reporter that his contribution to the project would be his memorial. Sadly, Henry died in 1975, before the contractors began reporting the paranormal activity.

Another ghost that haunts the Makens Bemont House is called "The Blue Lady" because she wears a blue dress. She is believed to be either Makens Bemont's mother, Abigail, or his wife, Pamela. The ghost is usually seen looking out a window on the second floor. A police officer told members of NEPVRG that he thought he saw someone looking at him from a window on the second floor one night while he was patrolling through the park, but he couldn't say for sure if it was a man or woman.

CHAPTER 19

Mark Twain House and Museum

HARTFORD, CONNECTICUT

IN 1870 THE AMERICAN WRITER, MARK TWAIN (aka Samuel Clemens) published his first collection of stories entitled, *Innocents Abroad*. The book quickly became a bestseller and its success catapulted Twain's career. While writing his second book, *Roughing It*, Clemens decided that he and his wife, Olivia, should move from Buffalo, New York, to Hartford, Connecticut, so he could be close to his publisher, the American Publishing Company.

For their first three years in Hartford, the Clemens family rented a home called Nook Farm while they looked for a suitable piece of land on which to build a home. In 1873 they hired a New York architect named Edward Tuckerman Potter, who designed and built a home for them in the Gothic Revival style. Construction was completed in 1874. As Samuel Clemens's career as Mark Twain progressed and his wealth grew, he hired Luis Comfort Tiffany's firm, Associated American Artists, to decorate the rooms and entryway on the first floor. The themed rooms, complete with hand-stenciled trim that is made to look like inlaid mother of pearl, are truly something to behold.

The Clemens lived in this beautiful home for seventeen years, and historians believe that these were the family's happiest days. While in residence, Samuel Clemens wrote what are held to be some of the best works of American literature ever published. While seated at his desk in the corner of the Billiard Room, which is located on the third floor, Clemens penned *The Adventures of Tom Sawyer, Huckleberry Finn, The Prince and the Pauper, Life on the Mississippi, A Tramp Abroad, The Gilded Age,* and *A Connecticut Yankee in King Arthur's Court.* Unfortunately, hard times and a family tragedy would bring this remarkable time of prosperity and creativity to a sad end.

By 1891 Samuel Clemens's finances were in trouble. He had made some bad choices with investments, which left him with no other choice but to close up the house and take his family with him on a lecture tour to recuperate lost funds. What started out as a one-year trip turned into a four-year journey for him and his wife and their three daughters.

In 1896 Samuel, Olivia, and their middle daughter, Clara, were on tour in Europe while their oldest daughter, Susy, and youngest, Jean, were back home in Hartford. The two sisters were preparing to travel to Europe and meet up with their parents and sister when Susy was struck with meningitis. A telegram reached the Clemens family in Europe, informing them of Susy's condition. Olivia and Clara left for the United States as soon as they could, but Susy passed away while they were crossing the Atlantic. Samuel Clemens received a telegram reporting the awful news. The family no longer lived in the house after the loss of Susy.

The house was sold in 1903 to an insurance dealer named Richard Bissell, who made many changes to the structure, and by 1917 he began renting the house to the Kingswood School for Boys. The house was then sold in 1922 and made into an apartment house. Seven years later it was under the threat of demolition when a group of concerned citizens bought the property and repurposed it as the Children's Branch of the Hartford Public Library. For the next thirty years it remained that way with some of the rooms being rented out to help pay bills. Restoration started around 1955, and in 1963 the building was declared a National Historic Landmark. On its one-hundredth anniversary, the house was opened to the public as a museum featuring many original items and furnishings belonging to the Clemens family.

Jacques Lamarre is the director of communications for the Mark Twain House and Museum. Jacques was very kind to give me a private tour of the house, and as we moved from room to room he recounted some of the strange experiences that members of the museum's staff have reported over the years. The first ghost stories he told me about took place in the home's main entryway. Inspired by Samuel Clemens's trips to Africa, the entry way is paneled with dark mahogany and it is in this area that the ghosts of a woman and a group of small children were seen on two separate occasions by museum guides. The guides did not see these phantoms when they themselves were in the entryway, but while they were speaking to visitors in the East Asian-themed Drawing Room, which is the first room on the right as one enters the house. The fireplaces for the entryway and the neighboring Drawing Room share diverted flues (instead of a single chimney stack) that allow for the placement

The Library. The ghost believed to be that of Susy Clemens was observed
by a tour guide entering this room through the doorway at the right.

of a window above their mantels. One afternoon a museum
guide named Mallory was with a tour group in the Drawing
Room when she caught sight of a woman out in the entryway
pass by the interior window. The guide was standing close to
the Drawing Room's opened doorway and was able to watch the
strange woman, dressed in white, float through the entryway
and pass into the Dining Room. All of the visitors were facing
towards Mallory when this happened, so the only thing that
they saw was her shocked expression. Interestingly enough, this
female apparition appeared just as the guide was talking about
Susy Clemens.

The second sighting from the Drawing Room was made by
a male tour guide (his name escaped Jacques's memory) while
he was standing in nearly the same exact spot as Mallory was
when she saw the woman in white. The guide was speaking to
his tour group when he noticed some young children out in the

Museum staff members have caught sight of a female ghost moving quickly along this short hallway to the nursery.

entryway, standing at the bottom of the staircase. These mischievous-looking children kept waving at the guide as if they were trying to distract him from what he was saying. No one is allowed in the house without proper guidance, and these small children were definitely not members of the tour group. The tour guide did his best not to let the sight of these mysterious children rattle him, but he found that very difficult—especially since they were glowing. In a few short moments the phantom children disappeared without a trace.

The next room Jacques Lamarre showed me was the Dining Room, which has a Japanese flower motif in its design. When the Clemens family had company for dinner, Samuel would get up from his chair in between courses and walk around the room as he entertained his guests with amusing tales of his travels. The sound of footsteps has been heard in this room when no one was present. Before 2003 the visitor's entrance to the museum was through an area of the basement that is located directly below the Dining Room. One evening after closing, an employee named Rebecca was in the ticket booth cashing out when she clearly heard someone pacing around in the Dining Room above her. The museum was locked, and she was the only person in the building.

The Library is located right off the Dining Room, and it appears to hold the playful spirits of children, possibly the same ones that were seen on the staircase. These little sprites have not been seen in this room, but people have heard children giggling and felt their clothes, legs, and jewelry being tugged on. A guide had noticed that on three separate tours, during three consecutive days, visitors had their bracelets and wristwatches unfastened while they were in the library. The reason for this playful behavior might be due to the fact that Samuel Clemens spent many hours in the Library entertaining his daughters with improvised stories and make-believe jungle adventures in the adjoining conservatory.

The second floor of the house is where the family rooms were located. Susy Clemens's old bedroom is set up to represent what a teenager's room would have looked like in her time. People have seen a dark shadow darting back and forth in the area between her room and her parents' bedroom. A guide named Jason was in the Master Bedroom with a tour group when he saw the translucent form of a woman dressed in white float down the hallway and into the Nursery Room. Another staff member, Patrick, saw this same female specter gliding into the Nursery Room as he was bringing a group up from the first floor. When conducting a ghost tour of the house one evening, Jason and the tour guests were in the Master Bedroom when they all heard people talking downstairs. The museum only lets one group of guests in the house at a time for reasons of safety and security. When Jason stepped out into the hallway, he called down to whomever was talking on the first floor. As soon as he called out, the voices stopped. No one was found, and the museum was, in fact, locked and secured. Mallory, the tour guide who saw the woman in white on the first floor, had someone "shush" her from the hallway while she was in the Master Bedroom speaking to a tour group.

On another occasion, a security guard was on the first floor when he heard voices coming from the second floor. Knowing that no one should be in the building at the time, he went to investigate but found nobody on the second or third floors. There is a ghost haunting the third floor that is believed to be George Griffin. Mr. Griffin was an African American who came to work as a butler for the Clemens family and became a trusted and respected member of the household. One witness saw his ghost sweeping the floor. It seems that George was well aware that he had been noticed because he smiled and waved hello before he vanished into thin air. Some guides and visitors have caught sight of him standing behind tour groups in the Billiard Room. George Griffin spent many evenings with Samuel Clemens in this room, and his own quarters were located on the third floor. As mentioned before, the Billiard Room was also Samuel Clemens's office, where he wrote many of his master works. Clemens had a twenty-a-day cigar habit, so one can imagine how this room must have filled with cigar smoke as he sat writing at his desk. One night the local fire department responded to a smoke alarm at the museum. As soon as they arrived, they checked the alarm board in the basement. The panel indicated that the fire was in the Billiard Room. When the firefighters reached the third floor they found no fire, but the Billiard Room was filled with the pungent odor of cigar smoke.

CHAPTER 20

Killingworth Café

KILLINGWORTH, CONNECTICUT

KILLINGWORTH IS A WOODED, residential area, located in Middlesex County. The region was originally founded as the plantation of Hammonasset by the General Court of Hartford in 1663. The court created the town of Kenilworth in 1667 and named it after the birthplace of Edward Griswold, who was one of the first Englishman to settle there. Over time, the locals changed the pronunciation to Killingworth. The original inhabitants were mainly farmers, with some of them owning and operating water-powered mills. Those living in the northern end of town made a petition in 1735 to separate from the southern portion due to ecclesiastical differences. The separation was fully established by 1838 when the legislature incorporated the southern portion as the town of Clinton.

Today, Killingworth has a population numbering less than seven thousand and is governed by a small board of selectmen. Its residents enjoy a quiet, rural way of life within the town's thirty-six miles of unspoiled countryside. Anyone who enjoys the outdoors can take advantage of Chatfield State Park, which allows activities such as hiking, mountain biking, rock climbing, and trout fishing. One of the town's favorite hangouts is the Killingworth Café. Located on the rotary of Route 81 and Route 80, the café is well known for its barbecued baby-back ribs, cozy atmosphere, and good spirits. Very few people, however, know of the spirits that oversee the old place.

The building has stood at this location for 275 years and has served many roles in that time. It has been a stagecoach tavern, brothel, parsonage, country store, post office, and a speakeasy during the days of Prohibition. Research has shown that the building was also used as a stop on the Underground Railroad. Janet Violissi and her late husband, Ted, bought the building twenty years ago after it had sat dormant for eight years. The place needed attention and some repair work, but Janet and Ted knew they could make it work as a comfortable place for folks to hang out in and enjoy a good, stick-to-your–ribs meal.

No one had said anything to Janet about the old building being haunted prior to her buying the place, but it didn't take long for the ghosts to make their presence known. Janet said, "When we came on board the paranormal was everywhere." While they were conducting the renovations, objects would move, tools would disappear and then show up in unexplainable ways and in places where they just shouldn't have been. They would hear footsteps and voices and sometimes catch sight of figures moving through the building that could not have been living, breathing people. Janet feels the ghosts haunting the place like to supervise everything. She told me, "They are as nosey as can be!" A ghost has been seen from time to time, standing behind the bar in the doorway to the kitchen. It is of a woman, about

The ghost of a woman has been seen standing behind the bar in the doorway to the kitchen.

five-and-a-half feet tall with frizzy red hair and wearing a bonnet. People who have seen this woman say she looks exhausted and appears to be surveying the dining room. Janet has seen this female phantom too and feels the woman was someone who put her whole life into running the kitchen when the building was a tavern. She also isn't surprised that this woman and the other ghosts are haunting the building. "This is where they belong; this is what they loved. I can see myself in one hundred years, after I'm dead, standing in the same place."

No customer has ever been bothered by any of the ghosts that haunt the business. The ghosts seem to inhabit the bar and café mostly after hours. Janet will often find a chair pulled away from one of the tables or the seats along the front of the bar all askew when she opens the place up in the morning. The strangest bit of rearranging that has gone on in the café involved an old photograph. Janet explained: "Eighteen years ago, I went up to the church auction here and found this lovely oval frame with a woman's picture in it, a very pompous-looking woman as far as I was concerned, very Victorian. I brought it here and stuck it on the wall. Whoever is here did not like that picture. We would find it behind a bureau, in the back room, by the door, and I was blaming my housekeeper. I said, 'What are you doing?' and she would say, 'I know nothing about it!' It would blow my employee's socks off every time it happened. Finally, I just had to get rid of it; I gave it to another of my employees. Whoever it is that's here didn't like that woman in the picture at all. She must have been a local pain in the neck."

Janet and her late husband made the decision not to open the rest of the building as an inn shortly after they purchased the property. Instead, they made those rooms into their living space. Janet has since remarried and is living at another residence in the neighboring town of Clinton. She and her new husband are currently renovating the old rooms for a family member to live in. During the time when Janet and her first husband lived in that part of the building, the paranormal activity was a common occurrence. A dog she once owned would often behave as if someone or something was chasing it. The dog that she currently owns has behaved in much the same way whenever she has brought it along with her to the café. Another pet that seems to be aware of the ghosts is their forty-year-old parrot George. He lives in one of the finished rooms and has been overheard conversing with someone when Janet and her family are sure that there is no one in the room with him. He has spoken words that Janet has not taught him. One day, he started saying, "Beer, beer," in a deep voice. Another vocalization that George has made sounds like an impression of someone clearing his throat. Janet has since learned that a previous owner of the property, Fred Winkle, died from throat cancer. Mr. Winkle is believed to be the ghost that has been glimpsed at times moving about the upstairs rooms.

Not too long before my visit, Janet's husband, Ron, was working in the upstairs bathroom, which he had to completely renovate. He was in the process of putting up sheets of drywall when he felt fingertips tapping the back of his head. Because he was trying to hold the heavy sheet in place and drive the screws at the same time, he couldn't stop to turn around. Ron thought it was Janet teasing him, so he told her to stop it. As soon as his hands were free, he turned around to let her know that he didn't find being tapped on the back of the head while he was working very funny, but no one was there. The ghosts are constantly moving objects about and rearranging things. After I had been introduced to George the parrot, Janet pointed out the sunroom where she entertains friends and family. She mentioned that the knickknacks filling the shelves along its walls will sometimes be found moved about. When I asked her if I could take a look, she agreed, but asked me to please forgive the dust because she hadn't been in there for a few months. We had to step over boxes of belongings that were blocking the door to the sunroom and again Janet apologized for the mess that always goes along with renovations to an old building. After we entered the room, Janet pointed out a ceramic jug sitting on one of the tables and told me that it belonged on one of the shelves. There was no ring left in the dust when she picked up the jug, which suggested that it had only recently been set there. What was more disturbing was that Janet's hand had what looked like a smear of blood on it from picking up the jug. There seemed to have been a single drop of clotted blood on the jug's handle that was just moist enough to smear on Janet's skin. When she washed her hands we could find no cuts on her skin. As Janet showed me around we found other objects that had been moved. The beds in two rooms had their pillows, sheets, and blankets all messed up, something Janet told me happens all the time. She also told me that the holiday ornaments used to decorate the café will often be found pulled out of storage just before it's time to display them, as if one of the ghosts can't wait to see them put up. Easter seems to be a favorite holiday. Janet just wishes that the ghost who took her yellow sweatpants would return them; she really would like to have them back.

Spotlight On: New London Ledge Lighthouse New London, Connecticut

The New London Ledge Lighthouse stands one mile off shore from New London, near the mouth of the Thames River. For over 150 years, mariners who sailed in and out of New London's harbor had been beseeching the powers that be to place a lighthouse in this location to prevent ships from striking the dangerous undersea ledge. The lighthouse was finally completed in 1909 and is still in operation to this day.

Lighthouse enthusiasts consider it one of the most unique offshore beacons in America. Before it was built, the residents of New London made it clear that they didn't want an eyesore marking the entrance to their harbor. Instead of the usual conical stone tower, the light was placed atop a thirty-foot-tall, red-brick house, designed in the French Second Empire style, with granite trim and a mansard roof.

The Ledge Lighthouse, as it is known in New London, is thought to be haunted by a former lighthouse attendant. Some researchers have speculated that his name was John Randolph (or Randolf) and that he committed suicide while stationed at the light sometime in the 1920s or 1930s. The story says that he jumped from the roof of the lighthouse after his wife left him for another man. The New England Ghost Project has investigated the lighthouse and believes the ghost is actually a construction worker who fell to his death by accident, not suicide.

The ghost stories started sometime after 1939 when the United States Coast Guard took over operation of the lighthouse. To the coastguardsmen who lived at the light, the ghost affectionately became known as "Ernie." The men stationed here would experience all sorts of odd things, such as doors opening and closing, cups moving by themselves, and blankets being pulled off them while they slept. Radios would turn on and off, and the television (before the days of remote control) would turn off by itself.

In 1987 the light was fully automated and the full-time crews left the lighthouse. Their last entry in the logbook is said to read, "Rock of slow torture. Ernie's domain. Hell on earth. May New London Ledge's light shine on forever because I'm through. I will watch it from far away while drinking a brew."

CHAPTER 21

Whitehall Mansion Inn
MYSTIC, CONNECTICUT

Whitehall Mansion is not only a terrific place for a romantic getaway, it's also haunted.

WHEN DR. DUDLEY WOODBRIDGE DIED in 1790, at the age of eighty-five, the *Connecticut Gazette* printed a eulogy praising him "as a man of temperance, unblemished morals, and serious religion... leading an exemplary life of virtue and piety." Dr. Woodbridge was a strong political and civic leader in the town of Mystic, Connecticut, and despite his advanced age at the time of the American Revolution, he was an active member in the patriot cause. In 1779 the doctor served on a committee to prevent currency inflation throughout the colonies, a serious concern for any nation at war. He also owned and commissioned a privateer, the snow *Black Princess*, which was a square-rigged vessel armed with twelve cannons. The ship's master, Captain Crary, and his crew of twelve men sailed the waters off the coast of southern New England in defiance of the Royal Navy.

The Woodbridge men had been ministers of the gospel since 1492. Dudley followed the family tradition and studied theology at Yale, Harvard, and later Cambridge. For reasons that are unclear to local historians, he departed the ministerial profession shortly after he married his wife Sarah in 1739. It is believed that Dudley Woodbridge then began studying under an established practitioner of medicine in order to become a physician himself. Dr. Dudley Woodbridge did, indeed, become a successful and prominent physician. His practice was situated at his original home in Upper Mystic, which also served as a stagecoach tavern for many years.

Between 1771 and 1775, Dr. Woodbridge built a home for him and his wife, Sarah, to retire in, and they named it Whitehall. It was built upon the foundation of a former home once owned by Lieutenant William Gallup, whose father, Captain John Gallup, was a central figure in the settling of this region. Whitehall was more like a mansion if compared to the average American farmhouse of the eighteenth century. Some of the home's outstanding features are the high ceilings, gambrel roof, large attic space, and the massive chimney with its first- and second-floor fireplaces made entirely from brick. The outer walls were even insulated (nogged) from the foundation to the second floor with bricks. Dr. Dudley and Sarah Woodbridge lived out the remainder of their lives at Whitehall. The doctor passed away on October 4, 1790, and his widow followed him on November 11, 1796.

The homestead passed on to the Woodbridges' elder son, William. When he died in1825, the property went to his nephew

Lucy's Parlor Chamber

William Rodman, who married his cousin Lucy Woodbridge. The Rodman family held the house until about 1850. A man named Joseph Wheeler then bought the property in 1852. Mr. Wheeler had his share of misfortune during his time at White-hall. He unintentionally plowed up part of the Woodbridge Cemetery, and the town fathers ordered him to repair the damage done to the family plot. He later contracted tuberculosis and died in 1872.

His daughter Louise married Samuel Bentley, and their youngest daughter, Florence Grace, became the last person to live in the house as a private residence. She lived there with her husband, DeWitt T. Keach, until 1962. In the spring of that year, Mr. and Mrs. Keach received a phone call informing them that the house would have to be demolished to make way for the construction of I-95. Florence Keach felt the only way to save the house was to donate it to the Stonington Historical Society. She also gave them five acres of nearby land and $15,000 to enable the society to move Whitehall out of harm's way. In 1969, with the help of others in the community, the home was painstakingly relocated to its present location. Whitehall remained in the care of the Stonington Historical Society for the next twenty-seven years.

In 1996 the Waterford Hotel Group purchased the property and converted the historic building into the Whitehall Mansion Inn. The house is now surrounded by the parking lot for the large Residence Inn that is also located on the property. As one turns into the parking lot from Route 27, it's hard not to notice the stark contrast between the modern hotel and the colonial mansion. It all seems even stranger when one takes in the accounts of ghostly activity that have been reported by staff and guests of the inn.

Scott Barlow, general manager of the Residence Inn, gave me access to Whitehall. Scott has been working at this location for three years and in that time has heard a few stories about strange happenings in the old Woodbridge home. He told me that people have reported seeing dresser drawers open by themselves, drinking glasses fly off nightstands, and footsteps on the stairways when no one else was in the building. Scott said, "Me, I try to be indifferent to all this stuff, but I don't like to come here by myself because it kind of freaks me out a little, even though they say it's all benevolent."

The general manager before Scott Barlow was a woman named Carol. One afternoon she and the hotel's chief engineer were doing a walk-through of the inn when they found they could not open any of the exit doors. They tried several times, but it was as if something was stopping the doors from opening. They eventually had to use a hand- held radio to contact the main desk at the Residence Inn and ask for someone to come and let them out. When the staff member walked over to the Whitehall Mansion and tried the main door, it opened with ease. The chief engineer could find no explanation for this and it has never happened since.

Over the years there have been numerous sightings of two apparitions in the inn. One is a woman and the other is a young boy. There is no way to positively identify these ghosts, but the consensus is that they are the spirits of Lucy and Benjamin Woodbridge. Lucy was the only child of the Woodbridge's that never married. Lucy didn't die at Whitehall, but she did live here with her parents. Benjamin died at the age of twelve in 1770, one year before construction started at Whitehall. It is plausible their spirits do haunt this splendid house that was home to the Woodbridge family for more than twenty years. One morning a guest told Scott Barlow about something strange that had happened to his wife the night before. The couple was staying in a room called Lucy's Parlor Chamber, located on the second floor of the inn. The man's wife had been sitting on the edge of the bathtub when she felt an icy cold hand touch her on the shoulder. Scott said, "We don't advertise the place as being haunted. They had no idea the place was haunted, so when I told him the house was haunted he said, 'You're kidding me! My wife's name is Lucy! I can't wait to go back and tell her; it will freak her out!" A short time later, the husband introduced Scott to his wife and asked him to please repeat what he had said about the ghosts haunting Whitehall Mansion so that his wife wouldn't think he was teasing her. They both were thrilled to have had such a unique encounter with the paranormal and thanked Scott for sharing with them the legend of Lucy and Benjamin.

When Scott Barlow finished showing me the five beautiful rooms the inn has to offer and related all the tales that he was familiar with, he had to leave me and get back to the main office. He invited me to stay in the house a little while longer and suggested that I look through the many volumes of guest

Phantom footsteps are heard on these stairs late at night.

books for more ghost stories. I sat for some time in the common room reading entries made by past guests. The majority of them wrote about how romantic their stay was at Whitehall. I did come across the occasional comment about the paranormal activity. Here are a few that stood out for me:

February 1, 1999—A woman (signature unclear) staying with her husband in Benjamin's Hall wrote: *Last night while we were sleeping, I rolled over and just above the door near the fireplace was a white cloud that just moved away towards the corner of the room. My husband says it was lights from a car—it wasn't. The car lights don't even come in the room at all. He said it was my imagination—it wasn't. I know what I saw.*

June 6, 2000—A woman named Lori K. staying alone in Lucy's Parlor Chamber wrote: *I saw the good ghost that lives here move the lock on the door. There is a good and benign presence here. That's a lot coming from a scientist.*

Many of the guests mentioned that they had never heard of the Whitehall Mansion Inn and found the place by accident. Here are two entries written about one of the first-floor rooms referred to as Sarah Sheldon's Parlor:

September 20, 2000—Mrs. A. W. Elliot wrote: *Had a great stay! Picked it at random from a list provided by a hotel that was fully booked. P. S. Very unusual place.*December 8, 2000—Clift Barnes of Fresno, California, wrote: *I stumbled onto this gem by accident in the form of an inadvertently canceled reservation at another hotel. After reading all the entries in this book, I am surprised that there has not been more emphasis on the spirit that resides in this room. No matter how high the setting on the thermostat, the chill will not leave this room. Things got moved around in the room overnight and something brushed up against my check in the middle of the night. Cool!*

The Whitehall Mansion Inn is a warm and inviting place. Its five charming bedrooms still contain the original wood paneling and wide plank floors. Each is tastefully decorated with period-style furnishings, large canopy beds, and all have working fireplaces. If you spend the night at Whitehall with someone special, chances are you will experience something supernatural.

Ghosthunting
Travel Guide

AMERICA'S
HAUNTED ROAD TRIP

Visiting Haunted Sites

All the haunted sites in this book are open to the public, and most charge no fees. You may wish to have a meal or at least a drink in the bars and restaurants listed. Also, many of them are included on the ghost tours in the area. Especially for families, the ghost tours provide a fun, relaxed, and nonthreatening way to experience paranormal activity. Don't forget to call ahead to make sure the site you want to visit is open, and make sure you call to make reservations for ghost tours, especially during tourist season.

MASSACHUSETTS

The Inn at Duck Creeke – Wellfleet
70 Main Street, Box 364, Wellfleet, MA 02667
Phone: (508) 349-9333
Desk Hours: 8 a.m. to 8 p.m.
Email: info@innatduckcreeke.com
Website: innatduckcreeke.com

The Fearing Tavern Museum – Wareham
Elm Street, Wareham, MA 02571
Phone: (508) 295-6839
Tours run every Saturday and Sunday through the end of August from 1
    p.m.–4 p.m. A donation of $3 is requested while children 12 and under
    are free. For more details, call Carolyn McMorrow: (508) 273-0069
    (President of the Historical Society).

Lizzie Borden Bed-and-Breakfast/Museum – Fall River
92 Second Street, Fall River, MA 02721 (For GPS: 230 Second Street)
Phone: (508) 675-7333
Email: info@lizzie-borden.com
Website: lizzie-borden.com

USS *Salem* – Quincy
United States Naval Shipbuilding Museum
739 Washington Street, Quincy, MA 02169
Phone: (617) 479-7900
Email: webteam@uss-salem.org
Website: uss-salem.org

Stone's Public House – Ashland
179 Main Street Ashland, MA 01721
Phone: (508) 881-1778
Website: stonespublichouse.com

The Groton Inn – Groton
128 Main Street, Groton, MA 01450
Phone: (978) 448-5614
Website: grotonstagecoachinn.com
Note: The Groton Inn was destroyed by fire just after this book was printed.

The Victorian – Gardner
4 West Broadway, Gardner, MA 01440
Phone: (781) 866-3435
Email: silentwolfproductionsco@yahoo.com
Website: hauntedvictorian.com

The Houghton Mansion – North Adams
172 Church Street, North Adams, MA 01247
For information, contact Josh Mantello:
Email: jmantello@msn.com
Phone: (413) 652-0324
Website: houghton-mansion.tripod.com

Ventfort Hall Mansion and Gilded Age Museum – Lenox
104 Walker Street, Lenox, MA 01240
Phone: (413) 637-3206
Website: gildedage.org

Rhode Island

Quonset Air Museum – Davisville
488 Eccleston Avenue, North Kingston, RI 02852
Phone: (401) 294-9540
Website: theqam.org

Slater Mill Museum – Pawtucket
67 Roosevelt Avenue, Pawtucket, RI 02860
Phone: (401) 725-8638
Email: info@slatermill.org
Website: slatermill.org

St. Ann Arts and Cultural Center
84 Cumberland Street, Woonsocket, RI 02895
Phone: (401) 356-0713
Email: stannartsctr@aol.com
Website: stannartsctr.org

Tavern on Main – Chepachet
1157 Putnam Pike, Chepachet, RI 02814
Phone: (401) 710-9788
Website: tavernonmainri.com

Stillwater Antiques – Greenville
711 Putnam Pike, Greenville, RI 02828
Phone: (401) 949-4999
Open daily 10 a.m.–5 p.m.

Connecticut

Captain Grant's, 1754 – Preston
109-111 Route 2A, Preston, CT 06365
Phone: (800) 982-1772 or (860) 887-7589
Email: stay@captaingrants.com
Website: captaingrants.com

Nathan Hale Homestead – Coventry
2299 South Street, Coventry, CT 06238
Phone: (860) 742-6917
Email: hale@ctlandmarks.org
Website: ctlandmarks.org/index.php?page=nathan-hale-homestead

Boothe Memorial Park and Museum – Stratford
5774 Main Street, Stratford, CT 06614
Website: boothememorialpark.org
Open year-round and free of charge

Abigail's Grille and Wine Bar – Simsbury
4 Hartford Road, Simsbury, CT 06089
Phone: (860) 264-1580
Website: abigailsgrill.com

Mark Twain House and Museum
351 Farmington Avenue, Hartford, CT 06105
Phone: (860) 247-0998
Website: marktwainhouse.org

Killingworth Café – Killingworth
249 Route 81, Killingworth, CT 06419
Phone: (860) 663-2456
Email: killingworth-cafe@comcast.net
Website: killingworth-cafe.com

Whitehall Mansion – Mystic
42 Whitehall Avenue, Mystic, CT 06355
Phone: (860) 572-7280
Website: whitehallmansion.com

More Southern New England Haunts

The following locations have a haunted reputation.

MASSACHUSETTS

Becket: Becket Quarry. Visitors to the abandoned quarry report feeling a strong sense of uneasiness, and a hiker claimed he was chased away by an angry spirit.

Bourne: Sagamore Cemetery. Believed to be haunted by the ghost of Isaac Keith. Visitors report cold spots and the strong smell of cigar smoke.

Boston: The Boston Common. Two phantom Victorian ladies have been seen walking through the park.

Brewster: Crosby Mansion. Haunted by the ghosts of two women dressed in black.

Brockton: Melrose Cemetery. The ghost of a man has been seen near the memorial for the victims of the R. B. Grover & Company Shoe Factory boiler explosion of 1905.

Concord: Colonial Inn. Room 24 is said to be haunted by the ghost of Ralph Waldo Emerson.

East Otis: Knox Trail Inn. Haunted by a young Revolutionary War-era soldier.

Fairhaven: Millicent Library. Haunted by a young girl and an old woman.

Gloucester: Hammond Castel: Haunted by the former owner, John Hays Hammond Jr., a man who enjoyed Halloween.

Greenfield: Eunice Williams Bridge. The covered bridge and river are haunted by Eunice Williams, who was killed in the river on March 1, 1704, by her Native American captors.

Hadley: Porter/Phelps/Huntington House Museum. Rumored to be haunted by Elizabeth Porter and a young African-American girl.

Lowell: Boott Cotton Mills Museum at Lowell National Historical Park. Visitors and museum staff members have seen apparitions on the second floor of the museum.

Mattapoisett: Ellis/Bolles Cemetery. People have reported seeing ghostly figures hanging from trees in the woods behind the cemetery.

New Braintree: Route 67. A female ghost, known as Elsie, walks along the road in her wedding dress on April 21, the anniversary of her death.

North Adams: Hoosac Tunnel. Haunted by workmen who were killed during the train tunnel's construction in the mid-nineteenth century. People claim to have seen ghost lights and shadowy figures walking down the tracks inside the tunnel. No trespassing.

Osterville: Osterville Grand Island. Locals say the ghost of Hannah Sreecham stands guard over hidden pirate treasure.

Plymouth: Spooner House Museum. The ghost of a mischievous little girl, believed to be Abigail Spooner, has been seen in the house playing with the window shutters.

Princeton: Watchusett Mountain. People claim to have heard the spirit of Martha Keyes calling for her lost daughter, Lucy, who went missing on April 14, 1755.

Salem: Turner/Ingersoll Mansion (House of the Seven Gables). Haunted by many spirits, one being that of a little boy.

Sudbury: Longfellow's Wayside Inn. Room 9 is haunted by Jerusha Howe, "The Belle of Sudbury," who is said to have died from a broken heart in 1842 when the man she loved never returned from England.

Rhode Island

Bristol: Colt State Park. The ghosts of two young girls have been seen near one of the beaches.

Burrilville: The Sherman Plot. The ghost of Laura Sherman has been seen motioning to drivers on Wakefield Road as if she needs their help.

Charlestown: General Stanton Inn. Said to be haunted by General Stanton and a Native American.

Coventry: Nathaniel Greene Homestead. Doors open and close by themselves, and people have heard footsteps throughout the house.

Cranston: Sprague Mansion. Reported to be haunted by former members of the Sprague family and a butler who once worked in the house.

Cumberland: Tower Hill Road. The ghosts of a boy and his dog, a girl sitting in a front yard, and a little boy on a tricycle have been seen many times over the years.

Providence: The Old Court Bed & Breakfast. Guests and staff have heard strange sounds and activity on the building's third floor, mostly at night.

Smithfield: Hanton City. The remains of an abandoned Colonial village said to be haunted by the phantom sounds of horse-drawn wagons and whispering voices.

South Kingstown: Great Swamp. Location of "The Great Swamp Fight" during the King Philip's War. The ghosts of Narragansett Indians have been seen in the area where the battle took place.

West Warwick: St. Mary's Church. Haunted by the spirit of Mary Doran, who donated land for the church to be built on in 1844.

CONNECTICUT

Bolton: Gay City State Park. The ghost of a teenaged boy, murder by a blacksmith in the mid-nineteenth century, has been seen running through the woods.

Brooklyn: Old Trinity Church. The woods behind the church are supposedly haunted by the ghost of a young girl who was killed by an infamous serial killer in the 1980s.

Burlington: Seventh Day Baptist Cemetery. Also known as the "Green Lady Cemetery." The ghost is said to be that of Elizabeth Palmiter, a woman who drowned in a nearby swamp. Her smiling ghost is seen near the cemetery on Upson Road and is always enveloped in a green glow.

Cornwall: Dudley Town. Remains of an abandoned Colonial village that is supposedly cursed. People say that the dark woods are eerily quiet. Private property, no trespassing—police take notice.

East Granby: Old Newgate Prison. An abandoned copper mine that was used as a prison during the Revolutionary War and the Civil War. It is said to be haunted by the ghosts of prisoners who died there.

East Windsor: Jonathan Pasco's Restaurant. Built in 1776, the restaurant occupies the former home of Captain Jonathan Pasco, whose ghost is believed to haunt the building.

Hamden: Sleeping Giant State Park. A mysterious man in black has been seen near John Dickerman's Castle. When people have approached him, he vanishes into thin air. He may be the ghost of Edward Barnum (P. T. Barnum's nephew), who was found dead in a cave on the mountain in 1873.

Hartford: Harriet Beecher Stowe Center. Ghosts of a man dressed in black and a woman wearing a tan-colored dress have been seen on the second floor.

Milford: Charles Island. Many years ago, the Paugussett Indians put a curse on the island. Visitors claim to have seen glowing phantoms in the woods and ghostly monks in the ruins of a monastery that was abandoned after bad luck befell the brothers.

Naugatuck: Guntown Cemetery. Visitors have heard children laughing in the cemetery.

Newton: Cyrenius H. Booth Public Library. Believed to be haunted by the ghost of Mary Hawley, daughter of C. H. Booth.

Norfolk: Blackberry River Inn. Ghost of a "white lady" has been seen floating down the back lawn to the inn.

Pomfret: Bara-Hack. Abandoned nineteenth-century village haunted by the sounds of farm life and children laughing. Private property, no trespassing.

Torrington: The Warner Theater. Haunted by a ghost nicknamed "Murph." He is believed to have been a homeless man who broke into the theater to stay warm and was killed when he fell down a back stairwell.

Windham: Windham Inn. Historic inn (now private apartments) haunted by the ghost of Elizabeth Shaw. Elizabeth was hanged after she was found guilty of killing her newborn baby. Her ghost is also said to walk Plains Road.

Afterword

YOUR GHOSTLY ADVENTURE doesn't end here. Andrew Lake has given you only a taste of southern New England's ghosts. If you want the whole meal, you're going to have to head out there with him, roll up your sleeves, and hunt the haunts.

I've known Andrew for several years, and what's always impressed me about his approach is the seriousness with which he takes the evidence and the witnesses, and yet he still has a childlike wonder about what's behind the spooks and specters.

In looking for ghosts, we're exploring our past and our ancestors. We're also pondering our own inevitable future because each and every one of us is going to die one day—what comes next is the greatest mystery. In our present day, discussing ghosts and haunted places allows us to connect with our fellow humans. We share these stories with people we trust. We were fortunate that so many were willing to share their profound experiences with Andrew in this book.

Whether it's a Revolutionary War battle site, an old mill, or a public house, places hold memories. If you walk in with an open mind and an open heart, you may just catch a glimpse of who has been there before . . . and who might still be lurking.

There's no better way of seeing a region than through the eyes of its local ghostly legends. What you hold in your hand isn't just a guide to a few dozen haunts, it's a method for conducting your own legend trip in these locations and at any other haunts you find along the way.

Enjoy the ride!

Jeff Belanger
Author of *The World's Most Haunted Places*, founder of
Ghostvillage.com, and host of *30 Odd Minutes*

About the Author

At the age of eleven, ANDREW LAKE had his first experience with a haunting during a summer getaway in Scituate, Massachusetts. He has been fascinated with the paranormal ever since. From 1987 to 1996, he worked in the field of home health care as a medical equipment technician. While visiting patients' homes he would sometimes hear strange stories about the moment of someone's passing and the occasional family ghost story. During this time, he shared an apartment with two friendly ghosts in the historic village of Hope, Rhode Island. In 2006 Lake formed Greenville Paranormal Research in order to sincerely investigate and document reports of ghosts and the locations they are said to haunt. Besides working on his own documentaries about haunted New England towns, he has contributed to the radio programs, "Spooky Southcoast" and "Ghost Chronicles." He is also one of the cast and crew on Jeff Belanger's Webcast television show, "30 Odd Minutes." He lives in Greenville, Rhode Island.

Printed in the USA
CPSIA information can be obtained
at www.ICGtesting.com
JSHW031210120923
48167JS00003B/6